ROLLER COASTERS, REVOLVING DOORS AND REFLUX

REFLECTIONS ON 37 YEARS OF PUBLIC SERVICE

AL BRAITHWAITE

All attempts have been made to preserve the stories of the events, locales and conversations contained in this collection as the author remembers them. The author reserves the right to have changed the names of individuals and places if necessary and may have changed some identifying characteristics and details such as physical properties, occupations, and places of residence in order to maintain their anonymity.

Published by St. Petersburg Press

St. Petersburg, FL

www.stpetersburgpress.com

Copyright ©2022

All rights reserved. No part of this publication may be reproduced, distributed, or transmitted in any form or by any means, including photocopying, recording, or other electronic or mechanical methods, without the prior written permission of the publisher, except in the case of brief quotations embodied in critical reviews and certain other noncommercial uses permitted by copyright law. For permission, requests contact St. Petersburg Press at www.stpetersburgpress.com.

Design and composition by St. Petersburg Press

Cover design by Isa Crosta

Print ISBN: 978-1-940300-61-0

eBook ISBN: 978-1-940300-62-7

First Edition

FOREWORD

I am dedicating this effort to my mom, Nancy Braithwaite, who was a career Public Servant, as a School Librarian extraordinaire. She was an Elementary Public-School Librarian for the Commack, NY School District for over thirty years. She was also the President of the Commack Library Board of Directors, when they built the first permanent Public Library structure in our community back in the seventies (her name is still on the building plaque). She worked there part-time as well, in addition to serving the Public Schools of Commack, simultaneously for the last ten years of her life. While she passed away in 1994 from cancer, she underwent radiation treatments for three months leading up to her passing and didn't miss one day of work. Talk about a commitment to excellence. Oh yeah, she must have been bored with all of that because she started a publishing company the year AFTER she retired from the Public-School Librarian gig. I promised her that I would write a book before I died, because she wanted me to be an attorney, and I didn't become one. Since she was responsible for making me passionate about learning through reading, I thought that completing a book would be a great way to pay tribute to her. A perfectionist, passionate about children's

FOREWORD

education, and a mastermind on how to make Library skills fun…..she invented the "Research Race," which had Elementary school kids in Commack crazed about learning how to do actual research (silly me…..I thought Library was for the boys to run and look at the naked women in the National Geographic magazines), she gave away prizes to reward them and kept the motivation going by making a competition out of it. As a long-term result, the kids who had her for their elementary school librarian turned out to be the highest academic achievers when they got to High School. In fact, towards the end of her library career, she sold the "Research Race" to World Book. Work Ethic. Leadership. Brilliant. She was the greatest example of a Public Servant years before the term was ever coined by the mainstream.

Miss you, mom. Sorry this took so long.

I also need to thank one of my colleagues, who goes by the nickname of "GZ" (or "G-Funk," which I like better). He oftentimes encouraged me to share this story. He has also been kind enough to help me shape it, into what I hope will be an interesting read. I need to acknowledge his contributions and thank him, because I may not have completed this without his consistent encouragement and editorial assistance. Oh yeah, I forgot to mention his name. John Garrett Zeliff. Many thanks for all that you've done for me.

INTRODUCTION

About me

I have been a career public servant. After receiving my bachelor's degree from Eckerd College in 1979, and my Master's degree in Public Administration from USF in 1991 (it took me six years of driving from Madeira Beach to USF Tampa twice a week at night for classes, starting in 1985). Not knowing what I wanted to do for a living, I only knew that I wanted to stay in the area. Enter teaching, something I should have come to naturally, because of my mom. Enter Algebra, the only subject I was marginally capable of teaching to High School kids (made possible by the large percentage of kids that hated it). As a former College Basketball player, I was the co-Captain of every athletic team I ever played on throughout childhood, so I thought of myself as a leader. If you don't believe me (about playing College Basketball), look at the front page of the St. Petersburg Evening Independent (now defunct) Sports section on November 22nd, 1978. (Irrelevant side note – during its existence, as the afternoon version of the St. Petersburg Times, they used to give away the paper for free if the

INTRODUCTION

sun didn't shine for 24 hours before. History showed that they gave away the paper on an average of only four days per year!).

Anyway, my government adventure started in 1985, where a Summer Recreation job turned into a full-time Government career. I started in Recreation, moved into Finance, became a Director and Department Head (kept getting promoted in spite of myself, some might say) in four different cities, until I became a permanent City Manager in the last chapter (I'd been an Interim City Manager several times before then). Simultaneously, I had also been a High School Basketball Coach for twenty-eight of those years.

So, I've been a teacher, a coach, a mentor, a director, a manager, a psychologist, baby-sitter, analyst, salesman (kind of) and all that apparently sums up a public servant. I come by it honestly, mostly because of my mom's service to kids and to my hometown (Commack, NY.... exit 52 on the Long Island Expressway).

So please join me for the next hundred pages or so and enjoy the journey that was my career I'm honest about all things that relate to me, so if you don't find some part of this detailed enough, feel free to contact me......I am an "Open Book" (pun intended).

About the Book

This book is 50% Auto-biographical, 50% Satire, 50% notes from a career on the "front lines" of service in local government, and 50% venting (I always give more than 100%).

Yes, this is a story. Let's call it a story with a purpose. A cautionary tale as I mentioned in the title. I hope it will be entertaining for the reader. More importantly, I want it to serve as a guide, or reference for people considering a career in Public Service or even a change within their current career. Leadership is vital to those who want to have a career in management. I'm not going to tell you how to lead, but by sharing some of my experiences, you will hopefully learn what it looks like and why it's important. The same point can be made about training, which is vital for success in anything you do. I'm not going to tell you how to train, I'm going to show you why it's so important. You are always going to be in control over whether you take advantage of opportunities presented to you in your career, and throughout your life.

To further the point, I hope that reading this will assist you in learning some of the key features of survival needed to have a career. Certainly, many years in the public sector should provide a few examples of things I had to learn in order to maintain my career. Business acumen is not commonly developed quickly, yet it is vital to those who consider career advancement a goal, and it takes time (say about thirty-seven years?). Hopefully, you'll see that my career success may have been related to how I tried to develop that skillset along the way.

This book is NOT a judgment on actions taken by any one government (even those I've worked for). Policy direction in the municipal space is supposed to be executed by elected officials, many of whom have a vast array of interests, influences, and individual agendas. The actions taken by a government are usually unique to their own time and place in history, or at least in how they see it. Clearly what works for one city may not be appropriate or work for another. That is the beauty of local government, it serves the public directly and closely, more so than any other level. So, while I suggest in this book that the recycling business model doesn't work (as an example), it is not a blanket indictment about any city that has a recycling program. Each situation is unique, and the reasons for a having a system or program in place may make perfect sense at one point in time for a city and then not in or for another. If we all learn one thing from this stroll down memory lane, it probably is that these distinctions are okay. I always find it funny that, so few people answer specific questions posed on the trade association "List Serves" (e-Bulletin Boards) about how their entity does things. My feeling is that no one wants to be challenged for why they do what they do, or worse yet, be accused in a public forum of doing something wrong! In the over-

INTRODUCTION

arching sense, while I think business models in government are fundamentally flawed, the main premise behind "Home Rule Authority" is affirmed by the fact that local politicians making decisions locally works best, even if those decisions sound incredibly strange to academics and pundits judging from afar (not sure, but I think I just became one of them).

So, as if you were in a class that I am teaching, I ask that you "buckle up" for the ride.

First, I am going to discuss what makes working in the public sector so attractive to so many. Some may find that incredulous, especially today, but it's still true. There is a never-ending supply of people who want to work in the public domain. I won't do much to analyze the sanity of that decision, but we will discuss why it continues to be so popular.

Next, I personally feel that we all have standards that we try to live by, and we are all unique in what they are, and in how committed we are to them. I suggest that anyone considering a career in Public Service create a list of those standards, those rules to live by. I will show you mine and maybe that will provide a suggestion or two on those nearest and dearest to your heart. I feel that everyone should maintain such a list and live by those rules. Important to note that they are rules of your own creation.

The "Words of Wisdom" section is where the satire starts, although I am heartfelt in describing things about organizations and people that you will hopefully consider useful. You might already know most of these, but they should serve you well, in either case.

The next two sections are strictly my opinions about what is good and bad about the public sector, simply stated. I believe you will find them interesting, even if you don't agree with them.

In the next three sections, I attempt to provide examples of actual occurrences that tend to cause the conditions I mentioned in the title. Roller Coasters are synonymous with going up and down in an unpredictable manner, something that many organizations do frequently. Revolving Doors go in circles repeatedly, another thing that many organizations do, especially those that are led by rotating elected officials (because most have term limits). The very nature of the election process suggests that there are going to be consistent changes. In my experience, the more damaging revolving door is when it is in the City Manager's office. Interestingly, a revolving door in one (elected officials) area oftentimes results in another (the Manager's office). And, last but certainly not least, Reflux is a disease (one that I got early on in my career) sometimes caused by stress, and since it began with "R" and I suffer from it, I thought it was a good term to use to describe some of the stressful situations you'll find in public organization life. And no, it does NOT mean that you will get it if you take on a career in Public Service.

Down the home stretch, I present reflections from things that occurred during my career. I hope you find these very helpful, and that you can use them in deliberating over whether a career in Public Service might be for you. These are things that happened to me, some happy, some not so happy, some good, some not so good. But they happened….and I survived.

Remember, survival in life has a lot to do with how you handle what happens to you. It's great if you can avoid mistakes, but in the public sector, and now with social media, everyone has an instant opinion on everything you do, so how you react can be as important as being proactive. Certainly, being proactive is probably better, but these days, almost impossible.

Lastly, I provide free advice for organizations, and more importantly, for people. Let's call them take-aways for you to use in your deliberations. None of them are overly complex (was going to say "rocket science"), but they don't need to be.

I'm not doing this to suggest that you implement everything I mention. I am providing reflections from experience, to try and help you decide things about yourself. If your ultimate self-reflection convinces you to do something else, then that is probably a good thing. There is nothing worse than wasted time in this life and if I can help you to avoid wasting it, then I have succeeded. Conversely, the same holds true for helping you decide that you want to pursue such a career. There can be great personal rewards

INTRODUCTION

about serving in the public domain, and it is a worthwhile pursuit. The point I'm trying to make here is that you need to decide these things for yourself, mostly by making a conscious effort to examine what makes you tick, what motivates you, what makes you mad. Not enough people pay any attention to this, and it has a significant effect on your mental health. Is there any more important subject in the world today?

I hope you, the reader, will consider the value to be gained from hearing about such a journey. I do not want this to be a textbook, but rather an entertaining look at the reality of what it means to be a public servant. I don't think too many professional trainings address the realities of this business (Reality TV isn't reality…or is it?).

Confessional – I was a public manager and, to some degree, an Accountant (don't hold it against me). The original book title was "Fifty Shades of Gray – Local Government Edition", and was selected for two purposes…first, to try and make this stuff sound sexy, so you would buy the book. Secondly, I thought that this title truly captured what is most harrowing about a career in government operations (the part about nothing being black and white…. hence the "gray"). Ultimately, I changed the title fearing legal reprisal from the authors of the original book. I have been told throughout my career that there is no such thing as bad publicity but decided I really didn't want to find out if that was true. The most fun part of this creation was thinking of the best title for it…. guess we'll see if the ultimate choice helped or hurt its chances.

THE ALLURE OF PUBLIC SERVICE

If you are considering the possibility of a career in Public Service, it's important to see it from every possible angle. Like most other things in life, the decision isn't black and white (that will not be the first time we say that). In Public Service, as in life, you should learn to expect very little clarity. "Gray" would be the best color description for about everything. In politics, that might not be news, but even in accounting, which was such a disappointment when I discovered that nothing was cut and dry, black or white, clearly right or wrong. Just think of how the investors of Enron felt when they learned that there were multiple methods of revenue recognition being deployed by those responsible for financial reporting. And, as it turned out, illegally. Apparently, even the law is gray.

This is a story.... kind of. I want to present the many sides of the decisions you need to consider if you choose to pursue a career in Public Service. Some good, some not so good. If the career chooses you, then so be it. By reading this, you will be better prepared to deal with the entire spectrum of things you'll likely face in this line of work.

As a public servant, I discovered many things about government, serving the public, and most of all, myself. I hope that sharing this experience will be helpful to anyone considering such a venture, and hopefully a good read for those who might be just interested in the stories.

It is a noble thing to want to help humankind, and that might be the closest thing you'll find to something cut and dry in this whole book. When asked why one wants to work in Public Service, most everyone says that it is because they want to help people. There you have it. The first and only clear statement about anything you will find here. I'm not even sure that the statement is true, but it does seem to be what everyone says, when asked. Okay, we will accept that as the premise behind why most people choose this line of work. For me, ultimately it was the ability to avoid Sales as a career, although I never realized that there is plenty to sell in Public Service. More on that later.

I will present some stories from experience that have led me to these conclusions. I also hope to make some suggestions about how organizations could be more effective and responsive, while encouraging individuals to identify things about themselves that will help in career or mid-life decisions on a personal level.

We all have plenty to do (not me, anymore!), so I am very conscious of the need to make this worthwhile for the reader. If you know me at all, you should know that I try to be both informative and entertaining, not just in writing, but throughout life's journey.

The title is meant to capture three of the most identifiable things that have occurred during my career. They also tell a story. Roller Coasters describes a ride, usually a thrill ride.... not for the faint of heart (or stomach), and exhilarating (or terrifying) when experienced. In the Public Service context, the ride usually makes for a difficult career, in that the lack of predictability in an organization leads to confusion, mistakes, high turnover, training issues and dissatisfied employees. Politics usually causes this ride, so Public Servants need to be more than familiar with the cause and effect, even if they don't necessarily enjoy the features that make Roller Coasters so much fun in some personal lives. I know I didn't. If you thrive in this environment, then Public Service is absolutely for you! It is apropos to suggest that Roller Coasters can be fun or hell. In the Public Service context, they are both. What they mean to an organization where you are employed, or considering a career, depends. Perhaps the first of many times I'll suggest how valuable it will be for you to know yourself. If you do, you will be better prepared for such a decision, using the premise that even deciding against such a journey could be positive for your mental and physical health. Knowing whether that kind of environment works well with your personality will be a big help, especially if you end up choosing to pass on the opportunity to pursue it.

Revolving Doors are an interesting invention in their normal use and represent a description of one of many environmental characteristics that do not serve public organizations well, when present. For this writing, whether Revolving Doors refer to your organizational leaders or your position, suffice it to say that neither are productive or enjoyable. Organizations that have constant revolving leadership generally don't get things done, or at least that has been my experience. Whenever the big boss is new, everyone has a new set of rules to follow or adaptations to make, and you might be surprised at how rarely they are seamless, from one to the next. I mean, the job is the same, isn't it? That would be short-sighted thinking. The leadership position is so intricate that people who take it on are different characters altogether, from one to the next (myself included). To survive this kind of Public Service, they must have an approach to each day that is extremely unique. That could be another whole book. I chose to include it in the title because it describes one of the features of dysfunctional organizations that frustrated me, so I think its relevant. Ironically, I also think it's indicative of another pet peeve that I have about society in general. The creation of the Revolving Door was meant to address a need, one I'll assume relates to a busy building. Was it truly necessary to improve ingress and egress (government term) by having a series of doors continually spinning? What productivity improvement resulted, and did we really need it? I mean opening a door isn't that difficult, is it? I digress, probably just entertaining myself here. The pet peeve which has some carryover is that I oftentimes question whether something considered a technological advancement is really such a thing. I put Revolving Doors in that category, while also using the term metaphorically for the purposes of this book. The dual context is handy, I think.

Reflux. Esophageal Reflux (in my case). The reward for all your stress, and that's if you are lucky. I know many colleagues who weren't so lucky. Your body absorbs everything you do to it, put in it, or take from your environment. It feels like heartburn, severe, and once you have it, there isn't much you can do about it. I take medication, so that I don't get attacks, but that isn't what I meant about not being able to do anything about it. It's a life sentence.

When you realize you have it, that usually means you've now received your first tangible personal reward for working in a stressful environment. Of course, you can get it many other ways, but stress does many things to us all, and for me, I woke up one morning when I was thirty-seven years old and had what seemed like permanent heartburn.... lovely. I've had twelve endoscopies and I'm due for another. I added it to the title because it was the first tangible thing, I got to keep for myself once my career was well established in local government. You might be lucky to have Reflux only, hopefully not something more immediately life-changing or threatening. Let's hope not, anyway.

The attractiveness of a career in Public Service has always been there, although it may no longer be as magnetic as it once was. Predominantly, I am referring to Public Safety, which has taken on an entirely new trajectory for recruitment, because of increased pushback expressed in society about a tiny percentage of employees that should have been held accountable for their actions. This book does not attempt to address the myriad opinions about what has transpired over the past twelve months in that regard, except to say that the urge to serve the public in any capacity may be dwindling rapidly, because of recent world events. Anyone attempting to evaluate what they want in a career needs to include an understanding about their own personalities, should they decide to pursue such a path. It's impossible to ignore that Public Service has gotten more challenging, and in some ways, dangerous. The things you need to consider before deciding contain a whole lot more seriousness than ever before. This is an important point to make.

For the purposes of this book, we will assume that the things to be individually evaluated relate to ones' personality and commitments, as opposed to a determination about whether one would be endangering themselves by choosing a career here. If that is even a consideration for more than just the parts of Public Service that inherently contain danger, then no one should consider this as a line of work, any longer. It is real these days, though, so it needs to be presented.

This dilemma feels like the military, which is ironic, considering that the military has many operational similarities to Public Service, and would likely be considered as such. The point I was trying (badly) to make was that the most difficult part of a decision to enter the military is the thought that you could be exposed to deployment, where your life could be in jeopardy. If that is now true about Public Service in general, the world is in very bad shape. Let's hope not.

I also wanted to add a thought about the process that used to go through a young person's mind before entering either Public Service, or the Military, or both. The decision used to boil down to whether you wanted to go to college. If not, then Public Safety or the Military was usually what you picked (in the "old" days). How many people had any real idea that their prospects for surviving to retirement age would be statistically lower by choosing one of these careers? Most young people don't think of that when they are young, and they certainly are not afraid of it. These days, it seems as if it's more of a calling for those who choose it, than it is a way to avoid having to go to college. Also relevant is that time has proven all elements of Public Service, not just those in Public Safety, contain real life (and health) risks associated with them. I never thought I would say that, and I certainly never thought about it when I entered this field but reflecting on the multitude of recent world events has brought home the reality of those dangers. Is it all worth it? Ultimately, that is something you will have to decide.

After reading "*Who Moved My Cheese?*"[1] and "*What Color is Your Parachute?*"[2], you would have thought that I knew exactly what I wanted to do with my life. During undergraduate education, we spent an entire month in the middle of our Senior year planning for our careers, which was very helpful. Not in finding one, necessarily, but in forcing you to think about it. Might sound funny, but not exactly high on the priority list of a twenty-two-year-old basketball junkie (*see my friend Dirk Dunbar's great book, "Confessions of a Basketball Junkie"*[3]) who was interested in three things....one of them was women, the other two were a toss-up between basketball and more women....and beer (okay, that's four things.... kind of). Anyway, the point here is that it was a valuable experience to study the "process" (important word...more on that later) of researching the particulars of what you might want to do for a living, in addition to understanding how it might work. If you knew what you were going to do with your life all along, then you didn't really need this kind of training, but from what I've been able to tell, very few people took it seriously, and even fewer do it at all today. A point to be reinforced here is that studying the "process" is extremely valuable, and distinctly different from the study of what you might want to do with your career. Those who research the "process" comprehensively stand a far greater chance of finding the thing they want to do, in this writer's humble opinion. I have no idea why that is true, but I absolutely believe that it is. Understanding how the "process" works is valuable because many people don't stay with what they found on the first choice....and that's okay! Many people burn out in their careers mid-stream, so having a solid grasp of how to study that next thing becomes even more important than it was originally!

Sidebar – I was a High School Basketball Coach for twenty-eight years. It was a labor of love and did wonders for my mental health throughout most of my government career, especially in times when work wasn't going so well. Sorry, I digress.... I coached a great bunch of kids that were good athletes, better students, but very few possessed the dedication to play Pro or even College Basketball, and even fewer had the requisite skills. Suffice it to say that these kids were likely going to "make it" based on their intellect or academic accomplishments (meaning it won't be a career in professional sports), which is wonderful and far more important. That is a good thing.

One of the things that I regretted most about my transition into adulthood was not doing more to learn in greater detail about what to study in college, or what to do with my life, for that matter. I transferred twice in college, played basketball for all three school teams, and still got a bachelor's degree within four years. I survived but realized that researching career requirements would have served me well in many ways, had I done it before entering college in the first place. I regretted not doing more to study what my options could have been, had I researched more intensely on what the world had to offer.

During my coaching "career", I tried to become a counselor of sorts for my players, as they set their sights on their journey into college. I wanted to make sure that they didn't make the same mistake that I had made and just described. Not sure if it ultimately made much of a difference, but my intentions were heartfelt.

Ok, so we have established that it is important to try and study things about what you might want to do before you enter the labor force. It is not legally mandated, but it makes sense, and some of us lucky ones had it force fed to us during undergraduate studies, in one form or another.

Confessional – while I did have significant training to assist in analyzing my choices, ending up in government (after teaching Algebra for six years) was largely due to the discovery that I wanted nothing to do with Sales as a career. It is important to remember that conclusion relates to my personality, which is one of the premises I'm trying to express as a necessity for anyone contemplating a career in Public Service. In a nutshell, for me it was the almighty fear of rejection (and most guys thought that was only a problem with girls!!!!). After studying all the things that you'd have to do to succeed in sales, rejection was the most prominent feature of it all, as I saw it. To get that sale, you'd have to hear 99 rejections, we were taught. It came down to something quite simple for me, but the training was very valuable in helping me to discover that with my personality, I wanted nothing to do with it. I had to evaluate more than just what I wanted to do, I had to mix it in with a healthy dose of what I didn't want to do (Golf principle....when hitting a shot, you look at your situation, decide where you want to be, but you must also evaluate where you don't want to be.....and make a club selection based on that....good advice for careers, as well).

Okay, if you are seriously considering Public Service for any reason (let us assume that it has something to do with wanting to help people, for now), I think it would be valuable to see a list of things that you should consider about yourself before making that leap. I tried to make my list a positive one, in terms of what you should be or should have in your personal makeup to survive a career in Public Service. One of the overarching themes would best be summarized by suggesting that it will not be anything like you might think it is when studying the possibilities of entering it. You have been warned.

To get started, I sat down and came up with a "Code to Live by", which I would like to share. The importance of identifying this is because you will be asked or required to do many things during your Public Service career (if you choose this field) that you may not be comfortable with. That may sound innocent enough, we all know that we have bosses, and the choice is simple....do what the boss asks or go find another job. This is not exclusive to the Public Sector by any means, but in the Private Sector, the responsibility for the decisions usually rests with the owner (or whoever has the money or owns the stock). In the Public Sector, you are associated with the outcome of decisions made by the organization, whether you had anything to do with making them or not. And, oh yeah, everyone in the Public has an opinion about that outcome, and with social media, wants the whole world to know about it! Good times!!! You get blamed by association…. how nice! Even on things that you may have disagreed with…. told you, you have been warned.

As a first step, it is important to think about principles that you hold dear…things you believe in, that formulate who you are, and what you will stand up for. Even if your experience changes the list as you move forward in your career, it is an important exercise. My list of rules to live by is original and specific to me. I suggest that you create your own, based on what is important to YOU.

WE ALL NEED A CODE TO LIVE BY

At some point in time while growing up, you eventually realize that you must stand for something…you must "take a stand". Some people figure it out sooner than others, but just about everyone will ultimately conclude that establishing rules (or codes) to live by is a good idea. My advice here - the sooner, the better, although I cannot say that because I realized it early…I didn't. Use this as your first lesson in deciding on a career in Public Service. It took me thirty-seven years to make this one official. Your list will not be the same as mine, but doing it now will absolutely help you, one way or the other. It may not help you decide whether to pursue a career in Public Service, but it will serve you well if you do. I would venture to say that it will help you regardless of your career choice. "Know thyself" is a good core philosophy to embrace.

These "Codes" are not like New Year's Resolutions, although we all violate our own rules on occasion, just like most of us do with resolutions. Let us call them principles to use in declaring what is most important to us. I discovered that some people write them down, which is a great idea. If you are a fan of the long running television series NCIS, you know what that means

("Gibbs" keeps them in a shoebox.... great for portability.... if you think of one while out and about, just write it down on a piece of note paper, and when you get home, throw it in the box).

I am going to list the personal codes that I have tried to live by, because a conversation like this, with yourself, is worth having. The purpose of mentioning them here is the value in understanding you should have your own, or at least in developing a process to learn them as your career evolves. I will provide mine, simply to show you what they are, and hopefully provide a little insight on how they came to be. Assuming we can say that I survived a Career in Public Service, I am suggesting that these principles worked for me, and I think they would serve you well (even though I wrote them down later in life).

Most of these will sound common, but you might find a flavor nugget or two in there that strikes you. Remember, develop your own! Here they are:

1 - DO WHAT YOU SAY YOU ARE GOING TO DO....BE RELIABLE.... nothing more important in your career, and in your life. Going out of style, unfortunately.

2 - Tell the literal TRUTH......in over thirty-seven years of Public Service, I have never gotten in trouble for telling the absolute truth in any situation. There is really no need for "spin" ...leave that to the politicians. In fact, if the politicians honored this principle, we wouldn't have the need for what social media has turned into. On the flip side, practically speaking, knowing what society has become, politicians telling the literal truth would likely eliminate the debate over whether we should have term limits. Is that a good or bad thing? You decide...

3 - If you find a fellow professional who is a fountain of useful information, in any discipline, immediately befriend them, and never lose their number. One of the most beautiful things about government employees is that we all suffer from the same horrible assumptions made about our worth (or lack thereof) in the court of public opinion, so in general, we are very interested in helping one another. I found that to be true in every area of government

that I worked in throughout my career, but especially in government finance.

4 - Be the kind of person (employee) who looks for more things to do. The good news – you will receive plenty more to do. The bad news – you will receive plenty more to do. More good news – you will be highly regarded within your organization, and ultimately more marketable. More bad news – you will not get paid more for it.

5 - Think of yourself as a professional, every minute you are on the job. You are not making anywhere near what professional athletes are making, but you get paid to do a job. That makes you a professional. Act like one. All the time.

6 - Show that you have pride in your organization and in your team. If you have a problem with another employee, ask for a meeting with them, one on one. See if you can resolve the issue without it escalating to the point where either one of you need supervisory intervention. This one is tough to do, but it makes a REAL difference, and you will find it prevalent in the highest performing organizations. It limits festering of ill will between employees, subsequently cuts down on some of the gossiping, and usually moves a needle forward that needs to be moved forward. When two employees act like professionals, they rarely get all that each wants, but good things result…for the good of the organization. Remember why you work here? Another point to be made…because municipalities are closest to the people they serve, the mission and vision statements created through strategic planning processes almost ALWAYS include a specific reference to the actual community (in the statement). It is wise to keep that mission front and center on employees' minds. Most people claim to be working for one thing, and one thing only…money. While certainly true, those organizations that have employees who can state that they work for the good of the community consistently perform better in improving the lives of the residents they serve, and subsequently benefit in their own careers.

7 - Do not take offense to being criticized…it is going to happen. Regardless as to who does it, see if you can derive some-

thing positive from it, even if you do not think the person providing the commentary was right, or authorized to do it. Be bigger than you need to be, you might find something useful in it. Have a THICK skin. The number of times that you will be criticized by people who have little or no clue about what they are commenting on is seemingly infinite (most often that group tends to be citizens). How you handle that reality may determine the duration of your career in this business. In different words, DON'T take things personally.

8 - ALWAYS ask others to evaluate your work...in a TEAM environment, the best work product comes from situations where many sets of eyes have seen it. One of my mentors taught me this....even if you are ultimately responsible for the work product, don't hesitate to have subordinates review and critique it....as previously mentioned, more sets of eyes results in a better product, and you are including your team in the final outcome, which empowers them, plus you don't present yourself as being too arrogant to assume that your subordinates wouldn't be of assistance.....great way to be on multiple counts......thanks, "Boss" (she knows who she is...MB).

9 - Take the attitude that your approach to the job is to get better at it, every single day. Get smarter, every single day. Our Administrative Services slogan was "Commitment to Excellence!" Even if we don't achieve it always, making a commitment to the effort sets the tone and tells the world what you are about.

10 - Learn what to read/watch/experience to enhance your job skills...as importantly, learn what NOT to read or waste too much time on. Everyone is trying to sell something these days, so if you can develop the filter of understanding what will make you smarter versus what will not, you will make much better use of your time, and enhance your productivity, as a result.

11 - Be Friendly, but don't be Friends (thanks, Frank) – this one is a tough one for me to write, because many of my best friends have come from my work experience. Perhaps more so in the management conversation, this theme is necessary. You must be willing to hold people accountable to have team success, and if

they happen to be your friend outside of work, that gets much harder to do.

12 - Relationships in the workplace are a BAD idea……once you break up, then you are looking at each other every day… enough said (if you end up married, one of you will have to leave anyway, because of most nepotism rules, so we only address the part about you two breaking up). And yes, I know the metaphor that best captures this rule, but I wasn't going to say it. Figure it out.

13 - Realize the public thinks that they can tell you what to do, because they "pay your salary." There is a protocol for handling that kind of input, so learn it and stick to it. Reacting to advice you think is inappropriately delivered can get you in trouble (trust me, I know). You don't have to like hearing the "know-it-alls" tell you what to do and how to do it, but you will occasionally have to listen to them. Be well rehearsed in knowing whatever procedural response your organization has for dealing with these kinds of inquiries, and be ready to deliver the company line, whenever challenged. Be nice but be firm.

14 - It's OK not to know everything (thank God). If you don't know something, just say that you don't know. Good customer service usually results if you then say, "I will find out and get back to you." Then make sure you do exactly that! (Refer back to Rule 1 – Do what you say you are going to do).

Young people, more and more, tend to think they know everything. Usually until they get old enough to have kids of their own (personally or professionally), and, at some point, they say, "Mom was right!!!!" "Dad was right!!!" "My old Boss was right!!!" A wonderful moment for grandparents and managers everywhere, but only if the kids admit that they said it. You will, or if you have kids, you have already.

15 – All experiences have value – The kids (translation – anyone younger than me) I was trying to teach (lead) are the ones I used to see every day at work. I try to convince them to take the benefit of the good things that I have experienced, and especially take something from the bad. Learn how it will affect you in your

journey. It is a shame that kids are totally convinced that their parents know nothing, and their bosses are **all** useless. There is so much to be learned, that **all experiences have value**. If there is another generational thing that bothers me, it is that the younger generations seem to believe that less and less. While they might be right about the bosses often, it isn't until they become bosses themselves (or parents) when they realize how difficult that role can be. Those that realize it sooner are better suited to be bosses (or parents) and will be more effective as a result.

16 – Don't take yourself too seriously – it is not generally a good idea to try and convince other people how brilliant you are. In today's world, doing so usually results in other people looking for (and usually finding) ammunition to cut you down, especially in the public domain. If you keep it light, and don't act like everyone should genuflect in your presence, you will likely gain credibility in the team environment. If you are that brilliant, it will show, eventually (so I've been told…. never happened to me). This is especially useful in the management context. It is generally well received.

17 - Don't participate in Office politics or gossip…the more you talk about what's going on behind the scenes, the more likely it will blow up on you, somehow. There are very few water coolers left, so it should not be too difficult to stay away from "water cooler talk." I have recently learned from a younger colleague that 'water cooler' talk should now be referred to as 'zoom" talk. And this guy was an actual Baby Boomer! Boy, is he cool…?

18 - Wasted time and wasted energy are productivity killers… work on recognizing both and minimizing wherever possible (you may not be able to avoid that meeting that your boss has called………zzzzzzzzzzzzzzz). Covid alert…maybe a positive from the cloud of the pandemic, my organization found that Microsoft Teams or Zoom meetings have been very effective. Using less time in personally attending a meeting helps, and possibly even contributes to shorter meetings as a result. I like the focus created by the bubble feel that you are in while conducting a virtual meeting. The part I like best is the control you can have

over eliminating side conversations that tend to interrupt the flow of a live meeting. Enter Chat boxes, which are fine, because they do not get in the way of the actual meeting agenda. I know, the other cool thing is you can be doing other things during the meeting without necessarily getting caught (don't tell my employees that I knew). Finally, if you chose to wear no pants underneath your business shirt in a MS Teams or Zoom meeting, do so at your own peril....just sayin'.

19 - Be upbeat.... it is contagious!!!!!!!!!!!!! Attitude is EVERYTHING!!!!!!!!!

20 - Study, wait......KNOW the Revenue profile of the organization you are in, even more importantly, one you might be considering for a new position or opportunity. And remember the age-old Accounting Rule......LIFO, or Last In, First Out. It applies to people too, not just inventory! Most people have NO idea about the financial condition of the company they are considering a move to. Maybe Finance people have an advantage here, but you better know what you are getting yourself into, regarding the financial condition of the organization you join, or you may have just traded a solid position for a shaky one. It happens WAY MORE than you think!

21 – The GRASS IS RARELY GREENER - My dad used to say that changing jobs was usually just trading headaches, and he was exactly right. That was his way of saying that the grass isn't usually greener on the other side. The job SITUATION is the most important thing you must consider, and you cannot ever know too much about that. As you get older, you know more about what you can stand and what you cannot. The commute? The reputation of the boss? The hours? Travel? Training requirements? If you are considering a new position, research the heck out of it, like it was the most important thing you will ever do. It very well could be.

It is here where I find the difference between the Baby Boomer and other generations widest. I remember hearing in conversation that younger professionals do not feel like they should work anywhere for more than a few years. That is crazy talk to me (as a Boomer) and it has relevance here. For you, the individual, if you choose to seek other employment opportunities after a few years, that is fine, but my question is about what you give up financially in terms of long-term benefits in the process (pension, usually). For the organization, however, people leaving after a couple of years is devastating to productivity, training, and keeping the organization moving consistently forward. Ironically, high turnover could also be good for the budget, but I would argue that the lost productivity is more significant than dollars saved by hiring new people at the bottom of a pay scale.

Bottom line is this - know the situation inside and out if you are planning to make a career move.

22 - Managers.... sometimes, you must allow your people to fail (thanks, Bruce). Now, failure is usually in the eyes of the beholder (there are plenty of opinions about that), but the point here is that effective employee development is oftentimes the result of a bad experience, which eventually leads to good judgment. Future leaders can be nurtured under the right set of circumstances. Maybe this is the anti-Micro-managing paragraph. You do not want your people to fail, but there might be a valuable lesson in there somewhere that is worth the experience. This is another tough one, because there can be great unknown consequences from failure in the political arena, and there can also be significant economic ones. In most public organizations, where staying out of the press cycle is of paramount importance, the temptation to try and prevent people from failing is very strong. Especially amongst those of us that are a bit OCD (obsessive compulsive disorder), or so I've been told.

23 - The Boss is NOT always right.... but he/she is the boss.

24 - Whenever the Boss is wrong, tell him/her if the right set of circumstances present themselves (usually behind closed doors), but protect him/her in front of any others. And tread carefully.... not all BOSSES are looking for your input.... know your audience!

25 - NO ONE is bigger than the game (team/organization). NO ONE. The second you violate this rule, you are done. History

proves that anyone who acts as if they are more important than the organization or community they serve is destined for failure. In politics, that usually involves the press, but even in life, the more you act as if your "you know what" doesn't stink, the more incentive you give other people to try and cut you down. A GREAT organization is where everyone realizes this and accepts it. Nothing gets done by only one person, and everything gets better because of the team.

26 - Embrace the professional environment as if it were a team sport. I love team sports. The best part of team sports is "being one of the fellas." (Thanks, Magic Johnson). There is no better feeling than striving for something bigger than yourself, with a bunch of guys, gals, or both. The realization that a group of people are much more powerful in anything they attempt together than any single one of them are by themselves is the key. Another wonderful feature of being teammates is that they will have your back in a pressure situation. You are in this together, all fighting for the same thing. That is a great feeling to have, and even better one to be able to count on when you need it. Relish the TEAM approach professionally. It works. Nurture it, train on it, sell it, cherish it and demand that your people do as well. If you are the manager, the blame is yours for failures, and credit goes to the team for successes. Build a strong TEAM and both your organization and your career will benefit.

Identifying groups that exemplify all that is good about teamwork are easy to spot. Those teams are usually known as.... **CHAMPIONS or TOP PERFORMERS.**

27 – Don't beat yourself up. You will deal with plenty of criticism, so be realistic about it. Again, don't take it personally. Learn and move on, this is a long road, a marathon, not a sprint. You will gain nothing by continually beating yourself up. If a criticism has merit, you will know it (Rule #28). Forgive yourself, hope your bosses do, and move on.

28 – Don't lie to yourself. You always know the truth, even if the story is lost in a sea of "gray" .... some people say that if you believe something hard enough, it becomes the truth. DON'T

ROLLER COASTERS, REVOLVING DOORS AND REFLUX

DO THAT. Even if the whole story isn't known, make your decisions based on what you know the truth to be. So much the better if you tell the literal truth to the world (Rule #2), but even if you don't (it happens), make decisions that affect your life based on what you KNOW the truth to be......don't fake yourself into believing a lie. That will always come back to bite you.

Your rules may be different than these. That is okay. They may change. That is okay too. While they will not be the same for everyone, it will serve you well to have a set of your own, and if you do, then FOLLOW them as consistently as you can. Review them occasionally and make changes as necessary. Sometimes you need to be reminded of what is most important to you, and you are the only person that ultimately knows the answer to that question. If your paradigm shifts, then change your code.... it is okay. Ultimately, it is just a good idea to have it by your side as a reference, there whenever you need it.

THE COMMON GOOD

Part of the "Allure of Public Service" is the thought that you are going to make things better for people in society, or in your community. I think it's important to mention that part of what Public Service gets in trouble for most often is over-reaching. That isn't a problem for those that want to serve the public in their career as much as it is a problem for the organizations that employ public servants.

Government, in general, is supposed to be in the business of providing services, and occasionally goods (think water) to the public that benefit everyone in a community equally or proportionately. Also, the decision on services to be offered is supposed to be based on things that the public cannot be expected to do well on their own (public utilities, build roads etc.). I'm not totally sure why, but that presumption no longer holds true in society, as evidenced by the increasing number of private sector bids to take over what have traditionally been considered public sector services. It is now common to see private companies running public utilities and depending on the service or good to be offered, some private companies competing with the public sector. Not really a focus for this book, but an important thing to acknowl-

ROLLER COASTERS, REVOLVING DOORS AND REFLUX

edge, if only to state what has become the obvious.... the population continues to have less and less confidence in the government's ability to provide those 'common good' services, at a level that they consider to be acceptable and affordable.

Public Safety, Roads, Water, Sewer, Reclaimed, Solid Waste, Recycling, Stormwater, Library services, Recreation programs, Building and Planning Inspection, Code Enforcement, Environmental regulation, Streets, Sidewalks, Parks, Sports Complexes.... the array has become vast over the years. The expansion of this list has happened because of the public's demand for them.... the same public that derides most of what they provide, and the same private sector that continues to try and make money from offering those same services more effectively than governments do......so much for the common good.

I never thought of my purpose in entering the world of Public Service being to make a fortune, and that theory has proven itself out. But I did see potential for making a positive difference in a community, which can be very rewarding. Unfortunately, I think the public's perception of that concept has been slowly but surely disappearing. Not because Public Servants have stopped giving their all to make communities better, but because there are blurred lines about what services constitute those most appropriate for governments to provide. This is also made more difficult by the newly empowered (via social media), who easily gain an audience by criticizing anything they see as not being personally beneficial enough to themselves. Now, anyone can spout off about anything they don't like, usually without having much of a clue about the specifics of what they should know before expressing a fair opinion. This growing trend is going to significantly limit more and more young people from wanting to enter the field of Public Service. Without altruistic people that really want to make a community better, what are we left with? Most every single Public Servant I've met during my time have been high integrity, good people really trying to make a difference. In retrospect, it's easy to see why a few of them have strayed from the true path in this calling. This country is still far and away the greatest in the world, and part of the reason why is related to our ability and right to disagree on stuff. But I see more and more people losing the desire to be a part of this, because no matter what they do or how hard they try to succeed in doing it, the un-informed take every pot-shot at those who work in this field for a living, at every opportunity. It's a shame, because if government worked the way it was designed to and everyone accepted it, we would get the best and brightest of all young people wanting to make that difference in a community.

I have another example that I like to use, and it referred to education and its relative pay, which we all know is horrible. If we paid teachers an exemplary salary (say 100K), what would we get? The best and brightest of what society has to offer. Who would benefit the most from this? The kids, the teachers, and professionals of the next generation…. people would want to become teachers, compete to be teachers, and do whatever they could to produce more dynamic versions of themselves for the next generation. Even without this simple but expensive theory in practice, what do we have in American society? Great, selfless, passionate people who know what they are getting into, dedicating their lives to making kids better at anything and everything. Is there anyone who can honestly say that none of the major motivators in their lives was a teacher? Can you imagine what we would have if we made teaching the profession to beat all professions??

I make this point because I feel the same way about government, to a degree. People that pursue Public Service don't do it for the money, and I'm not saying that they should, but if society treated them with the reverence that they deserve for what they forego in the pursuit of trying to help their communities, we would have far greater competition for Public Service minded individuals, and possibly even elected officials, as a result. When the spirit of service is pure, the results usually show. As I leave this profession, I fear we are heading in the wrong direction regarding that trend.

WORDS OF WISDOM – PART I

(ABOUT PEOPLE)

1

EVERYTHING COUNTS

All interactions with people and/or machines can and will be used for you, or potentially against you, depending on circumstance.

This will lead into our conversation about social media, which really bites many young people, while pursuing their career ambitions. All because they didn't think twice about posting that wise-ass remark, or inappropriate comment online. If it is in the public domain, it "can and will be used against you" ...... ("Book 'em, Dano" ...lame Hawaii 5-0 reference for you Baby Boomers).

Unquestionably, you will not know whether something you do counts or not, and unfortunately, probably not until it bites you in the butt. Especially for young people, however, it is important to think of this NOW, and not wait until you've been bitten before you realize that everything you do and every interaction may affect something in your future. The better informed normally make the better decisions. Do NOT assume that you can be exempt from judgment with anything you say that is available for public viewing. If you choose to express an opinion on social media, it's out there and you better be able to defend it.

Another important point to be made here, that I think is relevant. Participating in social media carries with it a presumption that very few people realize, until it's too late. And it parallels one that all public servants must accept from the start (which I find ironic). With social media, you have NO presumption of privacy! How many people think of that before posting something? If that prospect doesn't bother you, then maybe Public Service is for you, after all!!!!

2

THE TRUTH HURTS

It's important to be positive about yourself, and it's never a good idea to beat yourself up too much (I know, we covered this in the Code to Live by section…. stay with me). This holds true in professional circles, and in life. It is imperative that you NOT lie to yourself. In local government, you get told about how bad or stupid or useless you are, and this happens quite often. No matter what anyone says about me, even if I have screwed up, I try very hard not to beat myself up. It's counter-productive and it's wasted energy!

No one knows your truth, but you always do (just like in baseball…. YOU know if you were really tagged out at second base). To survive at this kind of career, you must learn not to lie to yourself. Denying something that you know to be true in public is one thing…. not a good thing, but sometimes it happens, and that is okay. What is not okay, however, is when you lie to yourself…… remember, GOLF rules always! If you know you did something wrong, don't wait to see if someone finds out or calls you on it. Report it yourself and fix it. You will find that fixing or admitting it yourself almost always results in a better outcome for all. This is especially important for people who worry a lot (guess who), oftentimes about something that isn't even a real issue. You know, in this line of work, anything can turn into a political fireball, so longtime veterans of Public Service develop the "skill" of worrying about anything and everything, since any single thing could end their career. It's "par for the course." (Too much Golf lingo?)

The truth doesn't have to hurt, IF you accept that you won't always get what you want. It is the normal discourse in Public Service work. Negotiations, pleading for a raise, trying to convince your boss or a citizen on an issue, or even asking for more budget money. Management decisions that ensure no one gets everything they want are so common that I think it's considered a style. Silly me, I thought decisions were supposed to be based on experience, due diligence, intellect, and sheer brilliance (let's hear it for experience and due diligence…. apparently, I don't have those other two).

When you lie to others, you are usually trying to convince yourself that the lie is true, as if that is going to make it all okay, somehow. You know the saying, "it's not a lie if you really believe it to be the truth?" (I think that is a bad "Seinfeld" episode reference). Anyway, it is unnecessary in order to maintain your job in this line of work. Lying to others can eventually cost you a job or a friendship, but lying to yourself will cost you much, much more. The stress that comes with that burden gets bigger and bigger (since **YOU** know the truth), and if you reach a point where its untenable, very bad things that affect your health usually result. Your health ultimately determines your survival…professionally and personally.

3

CONVENIENT MORALITY

I have experienced many people in my career that claim to be guided by Christian principles, but they seem to only act like it when it is convenient to be so. Regardless of denomination or belief system, I am commenting about the fact that many people I've encountered during my career claim to be guided by a denomination or belief system that suggests morality can be assumed. It has been my experience that many people in the public sector present that as if it were a "calling card." Simply stated, I don't think you should automatically assume that its true just because someone in your professional circles makes a claim of that nature. Call me skeptical. I'd like people to prove their morality with action before declaring it with narrative.

On a personal level, I absolutely consider myself a Christian, and while I am not necessarily very religious, I deeply believe in Christian principles, and most definitely have a personal relationship with Jesus Christ, my Savior. In my opinion, morality isn't based on a specific denomination or belief system, but someone with a strong moral compass will tell you all you need to know about them by their actions. In the professional context, establishing trust is vital to organizational and team success, and any means of discovery can be useful in that pursuit.

One of my first bosses used to make hiring decisions that violated our own personnel policies, based on the belief (or knowledge?) that the applicant was a Christian. At the time, as a "rules" guy (most Finance people are), I was furious about this. As a Christian, eventually I learned to understand what he was trying to do, although I still didn't agree with the fact that he did it. I grew to understand why he did it. If you could believe someone about having strong moral values, regardless of what denomination or belief system they held, you would unquestionably hire a more trustworthy individual (so he thought), and that is something every organization always needs more of. Naturally, if they really had strong moral values, they would never lie about something like this. The problem was that the proof is in the pudding...... many people say that they have strong moral character, but act as such only when it's convenient for them to be so. Hiring people based on that expectation is unfortunately short-sighted, because of this reality. Too bad, because if you knew it to be true and it was, the hiring process would be a whole lot easier (and more successful)!

I owe the fact that I received entry into this business to the man I mentioned above, yet I struggled with many of the things he did, and even more so with the way he did them. It gives me peace to finally realize what he was trying to do. He passed a long while ago, and I owe him everything for providing me the opportunity to get into this business.

On every team I've led professionally, we always TEST new applicants, partially for this reason. How many people are great in an interview, yet have very few skills when it comes to the actual job? If we can't be guaranteed in our decision-making about hiring someone that has the most appropriate skills set, then how can we assure ourselves in finding the right fit for a position (and the team)? I don't mean any specific or required belief system, I just mean someone with verifiable moral values, who would likely be dependable and a good person to have on your team. Can you find that any and every time you want to?

Maybe my first boss had it right? I don't think saying you have strong moral values is enough however, for the reasons stated above....... we TEST for the skills set and hire the smartest people we can find. We rely on our instinct to try and find the person that will fit in with the team and the organization's goals. We need someone to come up with a Morals/Values test, where the hiring entity could observe an applicant doing stuff without them knowing it, to see if they possess the values we are looking for. Now there is a marketing idea!!! (Forget about privacy.... it's the public domain.... just like social media!).

The reason we need all this? Because turnover is a KILLER! (More on this later)

4
DON'T JUDGE A BOOK BY ITS COVER

A lesson for us all, but crystalized most in leadership positions, public domain, where everyone has an opinion about you. Thanks to social media, where everyone thinks that the world needs and deserves their opinion, rarely do people that hurry to express it have any real clue about the whole story whenever they do. For me personally, probably the most frustrating part of the job. I bought two posters for my office when I became the Manager. They said:

What People See/What it Takes – they were both pictures of a glacier, with the beautiful part of the photo above the water line, and the term "Success" meant to be the part representing what people see. Underneath the surface, the terms Hard Work, Failure, Doubts, Setbacks, Persistence, Early Mornings, Late Nights, Sacrifices, Courage, Action, Risks all listed to describe the part about what it takes. The part you see, the parts you don't. Very powerful and true, I think.

You may never be able to prevent people from judging YOU because of our society and especially since social media made know-it-alls out of so many, but you must learn NOT to make the same mistake about others. This one is a long shot, but we must start correcting this somewhere, so why not start here? As my college teammate used to say (yes, even then) ...." Be the change" (Thanks, Burger). In fact, he still says it to this day!

5

PURSUIT OF PERFECTION

I didn't realize it at the time, but one of the greatest things my dad ever did for me was to expect performance. If I got a 90 on a math test, I would be proud, announce it at home, to which my father would inevitably say, "why didn't you get a 95?" I think he was kidding…. he was…. kind of…. kind of not.

Next test, I got a 95, now I'd hustle home and announce it even louder, to which he would say, "why didn't you get 100?" Okay, I finally get 100, RUN home to tell my family, and my father, half-jokingly says, "why didn't you get 102?"

Wonderful motivator, especially if done with love. We all wanted to please our parents, so who better to determine the heights of your performance expectations? (For fear of what he might say, when I finally got a 102, I didn't tell him at all!!! Enough is enough…).

6

BE GREAT WITH PEOPLE

The single most important thing you will need to succeed. In your LIFE.

You may not ever know if you succeed at this, but you will certainly know if you don't.

I have a dear friend, who passed away a couple of years ago. His name was Jim McKean. A GREAT man…. what made him so? It wasn't until he passed that I was able to figure that out, and in doing so, I realized that it is likely the most important thing you could be in this world, no matter what you do for meaning, or for a living. That is to be **GREAT** with **PEOPLE**.

Jim McKean was GREAT WITH PEOPLE. He was famous in a certain circle of the world, but that didn't matter. If you were in the room with him, he made you feel like you were the most important person in the world, to him anyway. What a great way to be.

Jim's youngest son was on my team, and he was one of my assistant coaches during that time. We made many great memories. I'd like to share a few with you here. Here are some comments I wrote about Jim to his family when he passed.

AL BRAITHWAITE

A Tribute to Jim McKean – "#8" on your scorecard, "#1" on mine

I was looking for a quote that summarized what I wanted to say about this great man.... found it.

"**A life is not important except in the impact it has on other lives**." Jackie Robinson.

I'm here to suggest to you that by the standard as expressed in the quote that I just read from Jackie Robinson (and isn't it cool that a great BASEBALL player said this?), Jim McKean's contributions towards the lives of others, as evidenced by the incredible number of people who have paid respects in so many different ways, should be considered among the most important of anyone I've ever known. In the short time I got to spend with him, his humanity was indelibly stamped on my soul.

NOT because he was famous - Make no mistake – he was a celebrity, especially in the sports world.... we've all seen him on ESPN, we have seen him at MLB games, and for some who are old enough, you may have even seen him play in the Canadian Football League! But one of the greatest things about this man is that you also have seen him at CCC (Clearwater Central Catholic HS) and UT (University of Tampa) games, and all around this great community....as a fan, a regular guy, more than happy to talk baseball, football, hockey, basketball, and anything else with you, not ever giving the impression that he was any more important than whoever he was talking to.

Ironically, I first met Jim and Ann at a Hockey game, just as Brett was entering high school. It was during a brief stint for a minor league hockey team in St. Pete, the St. Pete Parrots, I think they were called (2002), playing at the Bayfront Center. He knew that I was a basketball coach from CCC, where oldest son Jamie played baseball, and I knew he was a parent of one of our many great athletes. Beyond that, we didn't know much else about each other.

Over the next hour or so, we discovered that we had a lot in common with our family backgrounds, the common denominator

ROLLER COASTERS, REVOLVING DOORS AND REFLUX

being Montreal, where he grew up and where my mom grew up. Hockey was a passion for me, just as basketball, baseball and football were for both of us. With Brett entering HS, little did I know that he was an outstanding athlete in more than just baseball, like Dad was. Oldest son Jamie was a great athlete, captain of the baseball team, so I assumed that Brett was coming to play baseball…. only.

At the time, I was the JV basketball coach. Somewhere prior to tryouts, I found out that Brett was considering a tryout for the team. Knowing how important baseball was to him, I was very excited at the prospect of having Brett as a freshman on what was to be my most talented team. Also surprised, in that I wondered if Dad would allow it…. I shouldn't have worried about that, because Jim loves his kids so much, but I'm sure he gave it some serious thought before acquiescing to Brett's insistence.

A consummate team player, Brett didn't DEMAND playing time, he just wanted to be on the team and gladly took any playing time he could get. Jim came to the first few practices, then offered to be my Assistant Coach, which I jumped all over, recognizing his great sports resume, yet not realizing all the additional advantages that his presence would give my team…. let me explain.

First one…. good for me, bad for Brett – Dad knew that Brett's future was going to be in baseball, and wasn't going to allow him to get hurt, jeopardizing his chances or the teams….so being around the team every day might help to ensure that. Well, if you've ever seen Brett play basketball……you might just realize why Dad wanted to be around….great athlete, great fitness, great energy, great man defender……polish….well, maybe not yet….in fact, I nicknamed Brett and another freshman teammate "The Saw Brothers"….."Buzz" and "Hack."

Brett's hustle and enthusiasm was a joy to coach, and I'm guessing he knows this, but Dad Jim would oftentimes tell me to take him OUT and let someone else play…. again, if you ever saw him play……totally fearless.

But here was the BEST part -

Assistant Coach Jim, whom, as many of you know, was one of the MLB Supervisor of Officials at that time, gave us an amazing advantage that I had never considered. At the HS level, Referees would not allow Assistant Coaches to stand up during a game, let alone say anything, without risking a technical foul. However, most of the Officials at this level were also fledgling baseball umpires, trying to scratch out a living, in hopes of someday becoming a Big-League Umpire.... ALL of them KNEW and WORSHIPPED Jim McKean. So, throughout the season, my Assistant could get up, walk over to the scorer's table, talk to the refs during the game or during timeouts, and for some reason, I didn't get ANY technicals that year, which was more than likely a first (and only occurrence). To further support what a great thing this was, let me share something that Dan Morrison, an accomplished AL Umpire who also moonlighted as a HS Basketball Official back in my early coaching days, once said to me, after giving me a second technical in a game......"I make a living out of taking sh** from American League players and managers, you think I'm going to take sh** from a High School Math teacher?" If only I had my assistant sooner....

By the way, we were 18-2 that year...

Jim's "humanity" came through every single day....and you knew how much he loved people. Over the next few years, Jim did many wonderful things for me and my family.... when he passed, I was devastated, but couldn't help but remember all the ways he was kind, and not just to me. If you were around Jim McKean, you were in the presence of greatness, but not for his fame, but for his humanity. I want to tell you all the stories, but we would be here all day. Suffice it to say that Jim McKean went out of his way to get me the opportunity to meet Scotty Bowman, the greatest NHL coach of all time, he got me on the field at Brighthouse (now Spectrum) stadium when it was first opened, he got my nephew a tryout with a professional NHL officials camp, to name a few of the wonderful things he did for me. Everywhere I turned, he was always doing something nice for people.

When hearing of Jim's passing, I reflected on the brief time, in the grand scheme of things, that I got to spend with him. During that reflection, every single episode that involved Jim McKean was always another example of how kind and generous he was, how incredibly well he treated people.

There will never be another Jim McKean.

BE GREAT......at what you do, but most importantly, BE GREAT with PEOPLE. In my job, I used to tell my staff this every day.... from now on, you should tell yours TWICE a day!

Jim McKean's biggest accomplishments were the quality of his offspring, and his humanity.

I resolve in my own life to improve on the lessons that Jim left for us all.... love your kids....and be GREAT.... with People. Those are the two best things you could be.

Of all the things you could be in your life, how well you show your appreciation for the people in it will likely determine your success more so than any single thing you are, can do or be.

Many people don't deserve to be treated with the kind of respect and kindness that Jim McKean exemplified. Your challenge is to fight through all of that and find a way to consistently show your commitment towards the treatment of your fellow man/woman. On some days, it's a massive undertaking!!!!!!!!

7

WESTERN CIVILIZATION (REVERE YOUR ELDERS)

The worst part of living in this society is that we don't listen to old people. They are the ones that have all the relevant experience.

In school, we almost always had to take history class, studying a primitive culture of some sort. I remember thinking of what a waste it was, you know, the same way that people suggest that learning math is a waste of time, because they are never going to use it in real life (total BS, by the way……we all use math). Anyway, I get it now……I was right about Western Civilization being a waste of time, but not because we didn't need to understand primitive cultures, but because we were never told **WHY** we needed to know!!!!! If the message was that we would finally realize that we should worship our elders, because of their experience, then that should have been the overarching theme on the syllabus (who am I kidding….it still wouldn't have worked).

In the organizational sense, translation here for me is to hold onto the old people any way you can…. they understand the mission, are amazingly reliable, and have all the experience you need to perform, every single day. Consistent with our goal of limiting turnover, holding onto the life experienced people can do great things for your organization. Make them teachers and trainers as well, to impart that wisdom to those that will inherit the responsibility of delivering the mission to the community.

Holding onto the old ones has one drawback, although most of you who know may be questioning my sanity for suggesting it. The claims experience of your health plan may take a hit but remember that most municipal health plans allow retirees to remain on it anyway (although THEY pay for the premiums, in some/most cases). Another underappreciated benefit is that our oldest work veterans serve as a built-in buffer against an age discrimination claim. Laugh if you will, but you won't be laughing if the EEOC comes knocking at your door. Even if you ultimately prevail, your organization will feel like it had an involuntary operation of an unsavory kind (fill in with your own adjective here).

I never understood why we throw the older ones away.... they normally have the most knowledge of history, something very important for continuity of operations. It looks like maybe I'm the only one that finally figured out WHY we all had to take a Western Civilization or Primitive Cultures class! In all these cultural examples, elders were revered, as they should have been. If good judgement comes from bad experience, doesn't it follow that the best judgement would normally come from those with the MOST experience?

We probably know why this occurs, now. Older people know the most about what their experiences have taught them. The only problem is that it takes too long for them to make the point! The stories that come along with the experience tend to divert the focus of the conversation. Confessional – now that I am one of "those", I'm writing a book to tell the stories! Ultimately hoping that you'll read it all, but essentially leaving the same choice to you.... a choice you might not have if in a live conversation with me. Aren't I considerate?

8

ALL THINGS CONSIDERED – OR CONSIDER ALL THINGS

You should consider all sides of an issue before making an important life changing decision, or any decision, if possible. Getting better at this is a learned art (normally through making bad decisions…. it's okay, you will survive).

Very rarely do career professionals favor thorough consideration of the consequences from an idea more so than the speed by which it is to be executed, ideally. Good news here, and that is because it isn't their fault. The Private sector may be worse about this, but Government is bad. You are always dealing with deadline, and when it comes along with every assignment you receive, you eventually start adding it as a factor to your process of making personal or professional decisions. That is almost always a mistake. There are plenty of things you must make a quick decision on, but it's vital to try and develop your analytical skills to the point where you know what factors must be addressed before making any big decision. This applies to work decisions, life decisions, and even work-life decisions. If you can, consider all options before making large decisions. Focusing on being productive increases the likelihood that you'll be able to spend more time on important decisions when you really need to.

In the career sense, and as importantly, you should also know when a decision has been made for you. Moving on when this occurs can save you a lot of wasted time and effort.

You may not know all things that will require consideration, but that doesn't mean you shouldn't spend time and energy in trying to research and analyze as much of what is needed as you can. Career mistakes cost in many ways. The better informed usually make the better decision. It's a DUH, I know, but......how many people do you know that have developed this art into a skillset????? They are called......SUCCESSFUL LEADERS.

WORDS OF WISDOM – PART 2

(ABOUT ORGANIZATIONS)

9

BIG FISH, LITTLE POND OR VICE VERSA

Let's talk about what the difference in organizations means when evaluated on respective sizes. Knowing your own personality, as we've now discussed, understanding the job situation is possibly the single most important thing you can do to help the chances of your finding success in a career. Is that career going to be in the government sector? One good thing to know among many is that defining small organizations versus large ones is a moving target, however, truly small organizations do business very differently than larger organizations do. OK, that's not profound, but think back to your ability to know your own personality and what kind of environment you would prefer to put yourself in. The difference between operational rules in organizations can affect you significantly. For example, smaller governments are more nimble and less bureaucratic, by nature. Larger governments have many more broad-based rules that have to be followed without exception. Neither one is in and by itself better or more effective than the other. But how that organizational process might affect you and your role in it is likely to be significant and it's helpful to understand the difference. And don't get hung up on the criteria that defines big from small, just understand how decisions will be made in each, and how that could affect you. To wit:

People earning management jobs in small governments are usually described as "generalists", and that is out of necessity. In larger organizations of government (and likely elsewhere), much more specialization exists, therefore roles tend to be narrower in focus. Translation for you is that both types could be of value to you in your career path, but you should also remember going back to knowing your personality, that being a big fish in a little pond may or may not suit you better that being a small fish in a big pond, even if you are in management in both examples. Also relevant is that technical knowledge (and perhaps a technical degree like Bachelor of Science instead of Bachelor of Arts) may lend itself better to the larger organizations, where technical expertise in a narrower focus of job duties would be appropriate. Generalists, by organizational design, are required to do anything and everything, simply because there aren't enough people around to do each individual thing. The difference between those two probably explains why I was able to have a career, so "vive la différence!"

10

"STUFF" FLOWS DOWNHILL

This is a common adage in most organizations, but perfectly suited (and possibly originated from?) the government sector. In organizational leadership terms, it correctly identifies the process by which the responsibility for resolving issues, especially problematic ones, permeate (was tempted to use the word "flow"). The irony, in case you missed it, is that most local governments provide sewer service (the "Stuff") to the community, and the transportation of that largely overlooked and un-appreciated vital service is based on gravity (thus, the "downhill" part). It's a fun saying to use because it does describe what may be a parallel to when the top person has a problem, everyone else (subordinates) has a problem, as well. I heard on a "Miami Vice" rerun once, the saying, "when the United States sneezes, the rest of the world gets a cold." These days that saying might be considered arrogance. To reaffirm the concept is simply to say that in leadership, sh** (the "stuff") does flow downhill.

Or how about, "when Elephants fight, it's the ground that suffers" .... not quite the same thing, but probably relates well to larger organizations, where the distance between management decision making and operational functioning tends to be largest.

11

FINANCIAL DETAILS

I know we've touched on this (see Code # 20), but this topic deserves some reinforcement. In the government context, a thorough study of the revenue profile, in coordination with an economic analysis of current society in your state, possibly region or nation, will tell you if the job is one where you should be considering an offer. In many more cases than you might think, it can be one where you should be running in the other direction.

One of the key parts to that analysis is how often the position you are considering is vacant. Repetitive vacancies in a position is a HUGE signal.... for whatever reason, no one stays very long.... could it be the Manager? The Council? The Community? The political environment? The Finances? The basic answer is YES....it could be any of them, or all of them at the same time. The key is NOT to make the mistake of becoming the next one to take the job, learn the hard way, and then have to move on quickly. That may not seem like a big deal to Millennials and most young people, because now it seems "en vogue" to stay in a position for no more than three years.

If you take a job , let's say for no more than three years, and it only takes you one to discover that there's a good reason why this position has been vacant so often, the time you've wasted will hurt your pension, your resume (maybe, or if you ask millennials, maybe not?), and your future unless you manage to find a position of greater responsibility and or prominence than the one you just left, by good fortune (in other words, luck!). It will also hurt your feelings!

The point to be made here is this: before considering moving on to a new position, be sure to read the comprehensive annual financial report (now officially known as the ACFR) cover to cover, regardless of what the position is. Also, find the most recent version of the budget and study it intensely. You will likely find many pieces of valuable information about the organization you are considering, and you might also find information that strongly indicates that you should not have anything to do with this organization. If you truly care about the longevity and quality of your career, and subsequently your life, that is.

There is a potential benefit to working in a difficult organization, but I can promise you that it won't be pleasant and won't feel like it's been worth it. The benefit is that your experience in being in an organization that doesn't truly serve the public the way it should, will give you a baseline of information, with the hopeful result being an assist in not making the same kind of mistake again. I speak of this from great experience, and even hesitate to mention why it was such a derogatory or negative environment to gain career experience in. For twelve years, my first twelve in local government, I didn't have a basic understanding of the political environment that existed at the local level. Therefore, I did not understand how providing services to a community was supposed to work. Because of my ignorance or inexperience, I spent my first ten plus years in government service learning how inefficient government operations could be, when the political arena is supercharged with self-serving citizens who, because of their life experience or job responsibilities, anoint themselves as experts for the community, even though government operations are thoroughly different than those of the private sector.

Sorry for the diatribe, but this section strikes a nerve with me.

My dad shared many times, the saying "don't trade your headaches", which meant to imply that you should not assume a new position would automatically be better situationally than the one you were leaving. As usual, his counsel was dead on, and I want to share this wisdom with budding managers and anyone who sees their future in greater roles of responsibility than they currently have. The whole concept reverts to the research element of what I spoke of in the prior few paragraphs. Doing your research about a position you're considering or applying for should help you in making the right decision for YOU. Final word here is simply this: don't be fooled simply by the prospect of making more money.

I'm not saying that money isn't important, nor am I saying that it isn't the biggest motivator (depends on the person). I'm suggesting solely that you make sure you understand as many elements of the new position as you can possibly research ahead of time, so that you make the best decision for yourself. If you are struggling to figure out how to do that, talk to your mentors and colleagues and see if any of them have ever turned down a position for similar reasons to those we've mentioned. Hearing about the plusses and minuses, or Pro's and Con's that led to a difficult decision is valuable, even if it is in the form of someone else's experience. You will gain confidence from knowing that other people have gone through it, and it is okay to turn down a position that offers more money because it is the wrong fit.

12

KNOWING BETTER

This book is about gray area, gray matter, about nothing being black and white. Organizations, especially political ones, operate by this overarching principle…. thriving in a career that exists within that framework is possible without necessarily requiring you to contribute to it, but you need to know that they ALL do (organizations). In fact, that is probably true about every kind of business in today's world. Somehow, I think understanding that you will encounter it should be beneficial. There is no need to be shocked or surprised by the discovery that nothing is distinctly black or white in the business world today. Get used to it, and how it should affect your thinking.

On a personal level, I should've known this was going to happen. I'm in Junior College, taking my first accounting course, and I finally found what I was going to do with the rest of my life!!!!!!!! Numbers! Business! Black and White! Debits/Credits! Math!!! This is for me!

After that course, I proudly told the world that I figured out what I was going to do with my life, and that I was going to be an Accountant (sorry, Mom).

After my second accounting course, in the very next semester,

AL BRAITHWAITE

I swore I would have nothing to do with accounting, ever again……reason was simple…. nothing was BLACK or WHITE (anymore)!!!!

Arghhhhh! How can Accounting not be cut and dry, right, or wrong, black or white? How can it be gray??????

I should have known. Maybe it's because gray is the color of everyone's hair that survives a career in Public Service? (Thanks, Elaine!)

ALL THAT IS RIGHT

(ABOUT PUBLIC SERVICE)

13

SERVANT LEADERSHIP

Defining Servant Leadership is many different things to different people (and therefore, not black or white.... once again!). A Servant Leader focuses on serving those people closest to him/her, more so than the organization, as a traditional leader might. Ultimately it is about creating a culture. Work environment, the air by which we breathe (and more importantly, serve). Creating a culture suggests needed change, which could be an additional book! To move leadership in the public domain back towards what it was always meant to be, we need to study the theory of how it **should** work.

Servant leadership is a philosophy by which the personal goal of the leader is to serve. The leader's focus is not the organization, as directly as it is existing to serve the people. In its purest form (when functioning as it should), this would fit our definition of what is right about Public Service. Why do we care about defining what is right about Public Service? I think it's important to identify what it is about wanting to seek Public Service as a career that makes it attractive. Perhaps it is better to say that when public service is operating as it should, its usually traceable back to leadership that is operating in this manner. It can be difficult to change an organizational culture (although I didn't have to do it where I was City Manager). It's an absolute necessity for survival in successfully executing the public's business during these trying times, more so than ever. As the definition suggests, it has a lot to do with humility and selflessness, with perhaps another portion suggesting that "process" is as important (or more) than focusing on outcomes.

I have discussed frustration with many colleagues over the common public perception that government is NOT functioning as it should, and that, in my opinion, is because many in leadership have forgotten why they are in it. Also, there aren't enough elected officials that regard their roles as public servants, which renders the manager's job far more difficult. If elected officials were taught or convinced to view their roles as they should have been, the functioning and effectiveness of Public Service would be a beautiful thing. Just like watching any team sport, when played the right way, it is a thing of beauty to behold.

Where you observe this beautiful thing only occurs when all team members work selflessly together towards a common goal. Call me old fashioned, but it doesn't even matter what the team sport is, when all team members are playing wholeheartedly for the good of the team instead of themselves, its beautiful to watch and always yields a better result! Heck, LIFE IS A TEAM SPORT…

Okay, have I just contradicted myself? Servant leadership is existing to serve the public, not the same thing as a teammate functioning for the good of the team, instead of the individual. Before you accuse me of hypocrisy, remember that I presented the example only to remind you how beautiful it is to watch a team or organization when they are clicking, all on the same page, working towards the same goal, objective, or execution of the mission statement. In the government context, that requires a servant leader, and it requires elected officials who understand their roles, without injecting hidden or personal agendas. The betterment of community results when everyone understands their role, and the focus is on "process" (see section on Process vs. Outcome) more so than the outcome itself. The "process" being the attitude of serving the public, which, when followed, usually results in better outcomes.

14

NOT SO COMMON, BUT ITS GOOD

When government is functioning as it should, then people's lives are positively impacted, usually by things that they cannot sustainably do by themselves or on their own. In its simplest form, government exists to provide goods and services to the public. Unfortunately, the measuring stick for the results are almost totally at the mercy of public opinion. Because of social media, society seems to have lost its focus on whether the "common" needs of the public are sufficiently being met, at a reasonable tax or user charge rate. Now, anyone who encounters any single item of dissatisfaction with a government interaction takes it upon themselves to let the world know how they have been abused, damaged, or hurt by the government's ineptitude. Then hoping to generate support for their opinion en masse, with the goal of changing the government's decision on whatever offended them. And, once again, when Elected Officials get in the way, out of their lane, the job for Staff, from Manager all the way down to the lowest paid Laborer, gets far more difficult. Let it be said that the best functioning governments are those where the elected officials understand the difference between operations and policy. Believe me, that is rarified air.

ROLLER COASTERS, REVOLVING DOORS AND REFLUX

Since this is a paragraph about the positive, let's try to bring it back.... when everyone understands their role, particularly elected officials, and performs it, staying in their lane, government can be very efficient and effective. Like any good team sport, it takes a village, and everyone needs to know their job. The decisions made about what will constitute services delivered for the "common good", are difficult, but when kept straight forward and basic, usually represent what is GOOD about Public Service.

ALL THAT IS WRONG

(ABOUT PUBLIC SERVICE)

15

YOU CAN'T HAVE IT BOTH WAYS

Sustainability and Economic viability – do you really think we can have both simultaneously?

A business model that works AND one that makes financial sense.

Sorry, millennials, these two do not often work well together (kind of like boomers and millennials). We must save the planet but doing so will bankrupt us along the way! Sorry, here is the government version....it will make taxes so high that people will move away from your community!

Without citing specifics (yet), this simply means that the public will oftentimes demand a good or service that cannot be delivered sustainably, from the financial perspective. If the public wants it badly enough, there will be some elected officials that will promise anything to get elected. Your goal as a manager is to deliver as many services as possible at the lowest tax rate. Quite a trick when you look at all the details. And remember, the overall goal is to make your community the most attractive to be found anywhere, so that people will keep demand on property high, which means tax levies increase because of home prices rising. If you are seen as not accomplishing this, the reverse happens. If many more people leave your community than come into it, your tax base can dissipate, and you will be left with financial disaster. If this occurs in your organization, you will certainly be affected by the "Roller Coaster" ride that it contributes to. If bad enough, your career might likely be affected by it, as well.

Not really the focus of this book, but I've long said that I don't care what economic development is in terms of form, but we should be desperately seeking (Susan? Sorry, bad Madonna movie reference) ways to make it happen, when and wherever we can. For those against it, their voices are important, for certain, but they will also likely be the noisiest of the complainers if the development doesn't succeed, and subsequently their taxes must be raised. It's a reality of life cycle, especially in local government. If you don't keep up, you lose economically. If you looked at St. Petersburg 30 years ago, you would have thought that they lost their way, trying to start a massive campaign on downtown economic development. High debt levels, high relative taxes versus the other nearby municipalities and what little development was generated moved at a snail's pace. Fast (or slow?) forward to the current timeframe......hottest real estate market in the United States, tremendous downtown offerings for culture, recreation, sports and entertainment. What did it take? Thirty years, and many elected officials that realized they needed to finish what they started. No matter what the opponents said or did.... that is leadership, and a necessity!

If you want any government function to be sustainable, you better learn the economics of it. Revenue growth doesn't come to government the way it normally does for business. With rare exception, governmental revenue growth comes from one or the other of two sources: higher taxes and/or economic development (which increases the tax base) ......let me ask you...which would you rather have????

16

THEMATIC HYPOCRISY

Government is supposed to be in existence to provide goods and services for the people, generally those (services) that would not be cost effectively provided by the private sector. That is the theory, anyway….

Private business enterprise is in existence to make a profit. If the product created or sold solves a problem that government has caused or created, then so be it. When it gets interesting is when the private sector attempts to offer a good or service, claiming to be more effective and efficient in delivering it than government does. This happens from time to time, usually whenever the government operation has gotten so full of itself that pricing levels convince someone who was affected by it that they can provide the same thing, at a better quality and cheaper price.

Let's break it down. Traditionally, the "common good" involves services that are needed by a community in its entirety. Roads, Parks, Sewers, Garbage, Water, Quality control over construction. Law Enforcement, Fire Protection, Emergency Medical Services, Emergency Operations response, and depending on where in the country you live, Education (some cities govern and manage the school districts that geographically lie within). In more developed communities, the Arts, Culture and Library Services are usually also offered to enhance the quality of life for people that choose to live there.

Today, more attention is paid to the priorities demanded by society in general. And, of course, no one wants to pay for them. Most relate to the sustainability movement, which needs to be a top priority if our grandchildren are going to have a world to grow old in. Renewable energy sources, recycling of water to eliminate discharge and pollution of waterways, recycling of solid waste to reduce or eliminate dumping of toxic waste into the ground, the water, or in some cases, the air. So, on the government offerings menu, we add Environmental regulations, and considerations (restrictions) added to everything we already provide.

First hypocrisy – each level of government, from Federal to State, and State to Local, have some regulatory authority over their smaller counterparts. It's very easy for the State, let's say, to tell the local government that they must meet a certain standard of water quality, established by politicians, with no assistance to the entity that is ultimately going to be responsible for meeting the standard (and paying for it.... this is known as a mandate).

Second hypocrisy – at every level where this is occurring, you should bet your lunch money that whatever regulatory standard is being imposed on a lower level of government has been created by a process that includes all the compromises that go along with politics. That almost always spells disaster. The Republicans want something, so therefore the Democrats don't want it...and vice versa. Doesn't matter if it is the right solution for the problem at hand.... little or no consideration is being given to that, which is beyond a shame. The 'common good' suffers.

Local governments shine brightest here, where the hypocrisy exists, but rarely does it get in the way of doing what is best for the local community. In Florida, we all should be advocates for a term you may or may not have heard, called, "Home Rule Authority." Read up on it, love it, live it, understand it. The State is trying to take it away, which is hilarious, because most people will tell you that State agencies are the least highly regarded of all government levels in their ability to deliver sufficient services, and their representative legislatures are currently in the middle of trying to increase their responsibilities, at the expense of allowing local communities to make their own decisions. Nobody believes that the State will perform the function or deliver the service with a higher quality, they are just mad because local governments generally have a better reputation amongst their constituents, and State legislators can't stand that (because they don't). The answer they've come up with not only ignores their own agency shortcomings, but it is also arrogant to assume that local governments should not be in the business of making law for their own communities.

The "thematic" part is simply this – the government theme is to provide for the "common good." The hypocrisy is in how this is delivered, from level to level of government, that affects some portion of all lives.

Does any reasonable person really think that a state government can know more about what people in a local community need than those in the community itself? If you've had my experience over the past thirty-seven years in dealing with State agencies, you would feel very strongly about this. I certainly do.

17

BUSINESS MODELS (IN GOVERNMENT)

They don't work. Economically. Few of them make any sense.... REALLY

First and foremost, the basic economic model of compensation for public employees CAUSES most of the problems that lead to turnover in the organization. Here's how and why:

You are a public employee for a small community – small community means less bureaucracy (good), but more people doing many different things, instead of specializing in something technical or specific (good for the person's career, potentially but likely bad for organizational effectiveness). We are used to calling these people "generalists."

Government compensation is determined by budgetary constraints (translation – tax dollars) so the opportunity to reward excellence in performance is generally non-existent, or at best, very rare and certainly limited (if it exists at all, it needs to be super creative.... another sign for you to watch for in your research on potential jobs).

Okay, over the course of ten years, let's say, employee "X" has a job and is awful at it, unreliable in doing it, and a lousy teammate. Until recently (generalization), the thing that most everyone claims to hate about government is that the employees will always have their jobs, they never get fired. Now, while that isn't as true as it once was, it is almost always caused by a weak supervisor who doesn't have the stones to deal with the reality of holding people accountable and getting rid of those who don't perform. It is here where the business model difference between public and private sector becomes glaringly evident. The Public Sector financial model requires no net income determination......the mission is to provide maximum services for the least amount of taxes and/or fees. If the "enterprise" doesn't make money one month, or for an entire year, no one "HAS TO" be let go. Therefore, over the course of time, many "dead wood" employees may still have their jobs.

Much to the chagrin of their fellow teammates, they continue to do as little as possible, yet they are still around. Naturally, the other employees must do more as a result.

Now, here is why this business model doesn't work.

Employee "Y", a real go-getter and team player, always asks if anyone needs any help, takes on special projects, really shines and is a wonderful public servant and teammate.

For years, this employee "Y" has been covering for "X" because of the pride they have in doing a great job. Unfortunately, after many years of doing this, they have not been rewarded financially for the exceptional job they have done. While a promotion is a possibility (and not always a good idea.... more on that later), "Y" is not being sufficiently rewarded for his/her great attitude, work ethic and results, as he/she likely would have been in the private sector.

After many years of this feeling unappreciated, the GOOD employee ("Y") decides they've had enough and goes to find another job. No doubt successful, they leave the organization, and what is left......the "dead wood" employee "X". See it now? Multiply this by the many cases that can exist in an organization, and what do you have left? A "Revolving Door", which causes many problems of its own, and the "dead wood" employees left to train the new people. Not a good thing.

Because the good employees don't get financially rewarded for outstanding performance (the government business model), the good ones leave, and the bad ones stay, making it even more difficult to provide great services to the public. That is the government business model and why it doesn't work.

Also ironic is the fact that almost every employee in the organization, if not fearing reprisal, could tell you exactly who the "dead wood" employees were.

Good news – employees don't get fired just because the organization didn't make money in a given fiscal period.

Bad news - the best employees leave over time, and the employees that have no ambition, are poor performers and should be fired are still with the organization.

Answer – Find ways to financially reward the top performers (don't fool yourself about every study ever completed about employee satisfaction….it may not ALL be about the money, but it is in the top two), be creative in financial awards, benefits and marketing the value of what you provide as part of the employment package.

Most importantly – hold the "dead wood" employees accountable and get rid of them if they don't meet the standard. If your supervisors don't have the heart to do that, then get rid of them as well. Effective use of the probationary period is an important tool in the management box. If you are unsure about whether to remove an employee from probationary status, DO NOT extend them! That is your signal, if it isn't working yet, it isn't going to. Very important point, more so for managers than fledgling public servants, but an organization that deals with accountability is always going to be a higher performing one. I hope that principle doesn't bite you somewhere in your career, but if you observe it in action, it clearly tells you something you can count on.

Easy to say, tough to do…….but necessary for top performing public organizations. They do exist, although I'll bet you that only LOCAL governments can really achieve that kind of status. Look for the most important statistic there is in the data metrics of local government......turnover. The best organizations have the least amount of turnover. Period.

Here is another example – Tiered Water Rates.

The goals that society imposes on government for the common good make it impossible to operate a government enterprise efficiently or effectively. To wit:

Social goal – Conserving Natural Resources/Sustainability

Method - Encourage conservation of water by charging more for gallons used beyond an established threshold, appealing to the consumer's frugality in the process (by punishing the lack of it in charging more for increased usage). The fewer gallons used, the less per gallon is charged (I suppose that is one way to look at it). Also known as a Tiered Rate Structure. If you view this negatively, you will refer to this practice as penalizing those that have a great need for potable water use. Keep your eye on the ball here, we are discussing why Government Business Models do not work, not the subjective opinion as to whether you like them, as they currently stand. What if someone has a legitimate use for more water? Bigger family? Visitors from out of town? So, regardless of the reason, you are going to be financially punished for using more than your "fair" share of the commodity. Who is to decide what "fair" usage levels are, anyway?

18

OTHER PROBLEMS

A – Net Revenue requirements – Government Enterprise is funded by user fees, also known as rates. To provide an essential commodity such as water to the masses, the utility constructs and maintains a production facility, thousands of miles of transmission or distribution lines and meters, to name the major parts. All these things need to be maintained and periodically upgraded, as required by other governmental regulatory authorities, **NOT** the utility itself. Translation is that the Utility has predominantly **FIXED** costs, that never go away, and don't change whether there are 10 customers, or 10,000.

To sustain that operation, user fees (rates) must be established at the theoretical break-even level, or more simply, so that the utility can recoup those costs, and operate…like a business (puking in my mouth here).

Re-enter the conservation rate table scenario…. the utility needs to have a certain amount of revenue to function/survive. If that required revenue is presumed to increase over time, the utility must raise more.

How? For the most part, their main tool is to raise rates.

On the one hand, the utility is trying to encourage people to use LESS water by charging them MORE for additional usage. Start to see the problem here? If the utility raises rates, the cost of every gallon will get more expensive, so it is natural to assume that people will use LESS water, because every rate table tier has gotten more expensive. If true (and it is), then overall consumption will be reduced, which will nullify the additional proceeds (revenue) anticipated by the utility in raising the rates.

In this scenario, one cannot assume constant consumption. If raising the rates does not raise sufficient revenue, then where does it stop? How can a utility ever operate at break even if it cannot predictably use its main funding mechanism effectively?

The point being made here is that the business model of the utility does not work, as normally structured. The imposition of the will of more and more people has created a non-viable economic situation for the delivery of our most urgent biological need. The reason I say it doesn't work is that you can't satisfy BOTH the sustainability needs of conservation and the viability of the business enterprise at the same time. CAN'T BE DONE.

B - Unit costs of production – Interestingly (or not), the utility production facility operates most efficiently (lowest cost of gallon produced) if it is being run at close to or near its capacity. Remember the previous comment about fixed costs.... they are the same, regardless as to how much or how little water is produced. If you don't sell a certain amount of water, the utility can't sustain itself financially. Translation – the utility would sustain itself best, which would likely translate to more predictable and possibly lower rates, if it were producing the MOST water possible for its capabilities. With an overarching conservation methodology, would lowering the cost of production be accepted by those who demand the conservation model, if it meant increasing the production of the commodity? For the reader to decide, but I think we both know the answer.

C – Ultimately, the problem is this. The customer demands a fair price for the commodity, and for the most part, doesn't want to pay for the fact that it is available to them at all. The utility must pay to construct, maintain, and upgrade the infrastructure required to provide the commodity to the public, but can only have a chance at recouping its costs if the customers use the commodity. It is a cycle that will never end. Painfully, it is oftentimes the people that are most vocal about the need for the utility to conserve precious resources that squawk the loudest about the rates being raised as a result.

If citizens want some control over the rising cost of everything, they might be better suited to accept a business model that makes sense. In fact, it would be way simpler to understand as well. There could be one rate, use as much or as little as you like, or need. Here is what it costs….in fact, dare I say, that if you all use more, it's likely that the price will be much more reasonable and predictable than it's going to be in the years to come……your choice. When the facility is used at closer to its capacity, then unit costs go down. If we weren't tied to punishing people for using what they need, would we have the rate problems we have today? Also, why make it the responsibility of the utility to punish those who choose to use what they really need? If the people are passionate about conservation, then let those be the ones with enough discipline to walk the walk. The costs of running the utility are not going to change because some people pay more for using less. I would argue that the opposite is the case, because of the point I made about unit costs when operating at full capacity. I can't help myself in mentioning the irony of the fact that the biggest complainers about the cost of the resource are usually those that have the least amount of commitment to the cause at hand. I find that sad, but amusing (now that I no longer must listen to it).

What's wrong with the reality of trusting people to use only what they really need? The laws of supply and demand will automatically make the price rise if the resource becomes scarce. That is a reality that we are going to face no matter what else we do in the meantime under the guise of presenting a concern for sustainability. Why is a volume discount considered okay at the grocery store, but not here?

Here is my final example −

Recycling – the big farce...the business model that is based on a lie.... another one that doesn't work.

Goal – Reduce pollution/sustainability/re-use resources.(All good goals)

Method – Recycling, into raw materials that can be re-created into something else that is usable, as opposed to being discharged into the environment.

Problem – Business model doesn't work.

Recycling companies do not recycle materials that are collected as such IF the price they are to receive for them doesn't represent a profit. Into the regular garbage stream, they go.... always have, always will.

Before you start blaming the recycling companies, consider this.... they have to do this in order to stay in business, because YOU, the consumer, would not be willing to pay whatever it truly costs in order to make sure that 100% of the recyclable materials actually get recycled. If you were willing, this problem wouldn't exist. You can't have it both ways.

Stay tuned, by the way.... this problem is already coming to the forefront (thanks, China) and will be dumped on your doorstep soon, if it hasn't been already.

Helping the homeless – this one is a tough one. There may not be an answer to this, unless society focuses on our citizens at home, exclusively as opposed to those that live in other countries......very difficult topic.

Goal – Help the homeless, those less fortunate than most, with food and shelter.

Method (localized example) – create a place, where homeless citizens can get clothes, meals and a shower. No work responsibility, come and go as you please. Not a shelter to live in, which is already provided at the County level.

Problem – This well-intentioned non-profit structure causes more homeless individuals to come to this city. Our city has become a center for homeless people, living in various man-made camps throughout the municipal boundaries. Our homeless population continues to grow and has more than doubled with limited data on numbers, several times since the construction of the building.

The County Shelter is within 10 miles of this community, and offers food, clothing and beds. One rule is that any inhabitant must work to assist in maintaining the services provided by the shelter. It appears that is the rub. The homeless that don't want to work come up here, get their food and clothing in our facility for free, then just find a place to sleep close by.

Our organization allowed the non-profit to use our land to build the facility and contribute a significant portion of their annual operating budget each year.

Result – more "Reflux" – It looks like a tremendously compassionate gesture on the city's part to provide for this facility, recognizing that homelessness is a real and growing problem, nationwide. The unfortunate reality for this community is that doing so has contributed to the number of homeless individuals that stay in this area. Are we helping to resolve the problem?

Last example, I promise –

Utility Taxes – society is moving more urgently towards alternative uses of energy, which is a good thing for the environment, potentially. Since Government is largely funded through an array of taxes that are based on your utility bill (let's assume electric for now), you should be able to see why Government would be AGAINST a massive move away from its residents doing anything that would eliminate their electric bill, since doing so would also eliminate the government's portion of its revenue "generated" from utility taxes……see it? Did you ever wonder why residential solar power just can't seem to explode onto the scene like we thought it would (or should)? The cost of the equipment is still prohibitive, but the government business model, funded historically (and significantly) with utility taxes (generally the 2nd or 3rd largest revenue in Florida municipal profiles), would be decimated if the solar movement takes off! If it did, do you really think they wouldn't look to make up the money some other way (hint – higher taxes)?

To summarize, society wants something that government regulates, and government can't afford to suffer the consequences of encouraging it as much as its residents would like. Why is it that only Private business gets to charge what it needs to in order to deliver a good or a service? The theory traditionally has been that the government has a monopoly of sorts on the good or service. I sense that those days are essentially over, or soon will be, by the time solar energy becomes cost effective for the consumer, or by the time that Tesla can produce enough energy (with battery cells) to become the power source of choice for residential Americans....stay tuned!

ROLLER COASTERS

Remember earlier I mentioned that working in a public service agency was oftentimes equivalent to the thrill of riding a roller coaster. Things that occur in an organization where policy makers are elected to lead (like a Board of Directors), and an appointed manager oversees daily operations (like a CEO) have quite a bit of ebb and flow to them, just like most roller coasters. While the thrill ride part is not necessarily a good or bad thing, I mean to imply that the effect of riding the organizational roller coaster will be stressful, although occasionally fun. The lack of certainty is the point to be made, and when you are employed in a public service agency, that stress will be part of your work life, more than likely. Here are a couple of things that contribute to the uncertainty of a career in public service.

19

HERDS OF CATTLE

We are taught as young students not to cheat. There is nothing honorable about someone who doesn't put the work in, takes shortcuts or tries to get something they haven't earned. That lesson IS important.

However, the functioning of Municipal government works on a slightly different scale, and one might say that it violates one of the basic rules we were taught as kids. It's okay, though, it's not evil, and it is explainable.

With the emergence of electronic Bulletin Boards, or List Serves, as we call them in Finance, municipal professionals can now share vital information about new laws, policies and procedures, or just about anything else they are facing. What is amazing about these communication platforms is how helpful they can be. Also amazing is how few professionals actively use them. Here's one reason why – whenever someone poses a question to the enrolled subscribers about needing help or an answer about how something is done or what something means, very few people directly answer the question (a pet peeve of mine in every context!), or if they decide to give an answer at all, it's vague and generally not very useful. The reason is that most professionals in local government realize that there are dynamic differences in how we all do things, and let's say that this concept is called "Home Rule Authority." No one wants to directly answer the question about how they do things, especially if comparing notes with the author of the request leads to being called out for doing things wrong, or worse still, illegally.

"Municipalities are like herds of cattle" …. conceptually, before making a Public Administration decision of any significance, find out what all surrounding municipalities are doing about the same issue. This way, you won't likely be called out for doing something incorrectly or wrong.

Plagiarism is encouraged, in a sense, in that we need to know what all others are doing before deciding what we will do. It's okay, maybe just important to acknowledge the assistance if you do take advantage of it.

Since all municipalities are in existence to do the same thing…. provide the most services for the least amount of tax money, sharing success stories amongst professionals is actually a good thing. Finding a winning formula for delivering a service or providing a program can and should be shared.

Maybe not technically consistent with the "don't copy" rule from our childhoods, but okay in most municipal contexts. The sharing part is also positive, in that it's good to have colleagues that are interested in your success.

Fear of bad press? Maybe. Fear of negative public opinion? Getting warmer. Fear of being the first to make a decision that turns out to be a bad one (in the public eye, of course…the only part that matters)? You got it…probably this one, more than anything.

I think it's refreshing, albeit rare, to find municipalities that are definitive about making significant decisions, without caring what other cities might be saying or doing. That confidence is usually a sign of competence, in my book. Maybe it's just the confidence that is impressive, but either explanation works for me. Strength of conviction. The roller coaster part comes into play because you will rarely find a public organization that doesn't oftentimes waiver, out of fear that public perception will be overly negative. Speaking of perception…please read on.

20

POLITICS – PERCEPTION IS REALITY

Poli = many
Ticks = blood sucking parasites

I once heard this adage, and its potentially meaningful for the good people of local government, while also being easy to understand. It refers to the business more so than the people who are in it, but it certainly does inspire its fair share of the worst part of Public Service.

Local Government works best, out of all the levels that affect us, directly or indirectly, BECAUSE political ideology has the LEAST amount of influence on operations at this level (or at least it's supposed to).

While elected officials make policy decisions, most effective local governments employ a Council-Manager or Commission-Manager form of government. The community pays for a career professional to run the daily operations of the government, and if the organization isn't too big, it normally works very well.

This may be a topic to explore in more depth later, but I would argue that there is an indirect correlation between the size of the government organization and its effectiveness, and another indirect correlation between the structure of the organization and its effectiveness.

It's not that politics don't play into any decisions made by local government officials, but for the most part, the manager is responsible to do what is right for the community, and at the smaller levels, elected officials are generally making policy decisions based on what they think is right, more so than whatever their political party has expressed as a preference......thank God.

During the election cycle, it appears that the party affiliation of each candidate is starting to become part of the process at the local level, and that is understandable, but a shame. Once elected, however, you don't oftentimes look at a decision rendered by Council and conclude that it was made based on party lines, like you almost always do at the national level.

Translation.... the result is that much more gets done. When it's good for the community, who cares what party it belongs to? Good managers handle that reality, although many do have their employment security affected by political ideology. Again, a shame.

Shout out to the County that I live in......much larger than all its municipalities, and therefore much less nimble in maneuvering. However, they must be given credit for handling the political nature of representing their constituents, with great skill. I can't say this about too many other counties, which, by nature, follow the rule I've suggested previously. But with great Administrative Leadership, and tremendous balance of intellect and savvy throughout the Board that governs policy, this County is a shining star in the annals of local government achievement (if there is such a thing). Since this County is the most densely populated county in the State of Florida (most people think that it is Dade), there is much to be dealt with, many people to govern, and not much room to govern in (play on words.... I think). The Constitutional Officers are exceptional, and politics, while in play, makes sense for the most part. Ours may be the only county I've ever known where I could say that. I think that is the major reason why I could never move out of it. Had many chances, couldn't pull the trigger. Forty-five years and counting.... but who's counting?

REVOLVING DOORS

21

BEEF TURNOVERS

When I was in College, I played for the Basketball Team...my nickname was (and is) "Beef". If you saw me, it wouldn't be difficult to see why. In College Basketball, all coaches and most pundits will tell you that "turnovers" are a killer (making an error with the ball that results in the opposing team getting it, without your team getting the opportunity to even get a shot off, which, naturally means that you don't score).

As a Co-Captain and two-year starter, it was important to show the team that I understood how important it was to avoid committing turnovers, because of their devastating effect on team success, and, in my case, because I was going to take some serious ribbing from the fellas if one of the cafeteria selections for supper that day happened to be "Beef Turnovers".....they tasted much better in the cafeteria than they did on the basketball court.

Anyway, that was one of the early episodes that made me realize how bad turnovers were in more than just the basketball context. Turnover in an organization is the most negative thing that can happen, and for some reason, it is still one of the most overlooked (and preventable, in my opinion). Productivity losses from high turnover is devastating to both organizational achievement and employee morale. In the morale context, nothing is worse than being told you must "pick up the slack" for a position where someone in your department or division has recently left. They always tell you that it will only be temporary, which is bad enough. However, when the next person shows up, guess who must train them???? YOU......I don't think the effects of turnover can be overstated.

What is the answer? How do we, or can we convince our people NOT to leave? Simple to say, not so simple to do......treat them well. Pay them well. Not easy to do in the Public Sector.

22

IF YOU GET "RUN"

Public perception is a funny thing.

Social media is a monster. It has created a medium for anyone who signs up to express their opinion on any and every subject without worrying about getting punched in the mouth for it. This statement is significant, and I mean it… think about it.

Public officials cannot make decisions in a vacuum. If that were ever true, it isn't any longer. Because of public perception, the damage is often done by the time that the truth comes out about a particular situation.

There is a significant chance that if you do ever get "run" (out the front door), it won't be because of anything you truly did. Of course, there are certain things that are unforgivable in every job, but once you become an administrator or higher, you are more likely to be blamed for something you are responsible for, not for anything you did to earn a trip through the exit door.

That doesn't matter, so accept it. Do the best you can to learn as much as you can about the things you are responsible for and live with all of what comes with it. The most important part to realize is that you will have way more on your plate than you will be realistically able to keep up with and understand that the interjection of personal agendas from those who hold your job security in their hands is what makes the situation impossible to master. All you can do is all you can do.

23

THE "GO TO HELL" FUND

My first City Manager was a great man named Ralph Rawson. He was a retired Navy man, who owned a business and became the City Manager after coming to Florida to retire. Of the many great life lessons he imparted, one in particular stands out. He would say that you need to establish your own "Go to Hell" fund.

The reason: sometime, maybe many times, during your career, you are going to be asked, or told to do something that you aren't comfortable doing. You may question its validity, or worse yet, its legality. Your boss is telling you that this certain something must be done, and you must get it done. Doesn't matter if it is coming from the Manager, or in many cases, the Council. What are you going to do? You are young, don't have much time on the job, and you are already being challenged to do something you think is wrong. The choices are to advise against it, which rarely changes anything, because you aren't able to dictate terms to your boss. You can execute the orders, as you've been instructed to do. Or you can refuse to carry out the instructions you've been given, at which point the "Go to Hell" fund comes into play. Because you are going to lose your job.

Know this…if you select a career in government, this absolutely **WILL** happen, maybe many times. Luckily for me, it didn't occur often, but if you think this won't happen to you during your career, you are sadly mistaken. Save some money, just in case, and don't make me say that I told you so.

REFLUX

Think of things that give you heartburn. Reflux, untreated, is constant heartburn. Most of us thought that it is related to something we ate, but you might be surprised to discover that oftentimes, it is related to stressful things going on in your life. Something you ate or drank is still likely to be involved, but the point here is that stress, in its purest form, especially over a long period of time, can cause Reflux, which is very unpleasant, and can be seriously detrimental to your health. It doesn't necessarily mean that it will be, but it could. Here are a few examples of situations you may find in the workplace that would likely contribute to getting Reflux. While there isn't a guarantee, I think it's safe to say that these episodes certainly contributed to mine.

24

SILOS

The analysis required to accurately determine what makes for a top performing organization requires a vantage point usually only available to those that work inside it. Each governmental organization has multiple departments, divisions, or cost centers. For the purposes of financial reporting, it is necessary to treat them independently, but for top performance, it is important to work together. When departments don't work together for the overall good of the organization, this is popularly known as "working in silos." The inference is that each department works only towards its own goals, and serves only to address their own needs, as opposed to the overall needs of the bigger team or organization.

Many of the most distressing episodes I've encountered with Reflux was because of this propensity towards not cooperating with other departments. Much like the effect of a Revolving Door in leadership, the existence of this mentality in an organization is poison! Worse still is that when it occurs, the negative ripple effect is usually glaring to the public, and that makes the entire organization look horribly ineffective. If perception IS reality, as we've suggested, then this is REALLY bad.

Nothing gets done, everyone looks bad, what could be worse

than that? The core cause, in this writer's humble opinion, is laziness. Many colleagues I've encountered over the years seemed to be most concerned about protecting their little corner of the earth, making sure that no one outside their departmental suite door knew what they were (or weren't) doing, and ultimately doing as little as possible. We used to have a saying about one colleague that suggested that they spent more time and energy in trying to get out of working collaboratively than it would have required to do the actual work…. not good.

25

MEDIA 1, TRUTH 0 - NOT EVEN CLOSE

It's Super Bowl weekend, 2021.... extra special time for Tampa Bay fans, because, for the first time in NFL history, a team has a home game for the Super Bowl. Made even more special because the greatest Quarterback in NFL history made it happen for what has traditionally been an underachieving team, apart from one year earlier in the new millennium, when they won the Super Bowl. Oh yeah, all this at the age of 43......dang, old guys are great! Anyway....

On Saturday morning, February 6th, 2021, I get a phone call from my Public Works Director, notifying me that for the past 12-18 hours, our ROWTP Staff has been inundated with interviews, from Law Enforcement and US Regulatory agencies, all because one Operator saw what was thought to be an unwelcomed intrusion, apparently someone trying to "hack" into the Plant operating software, attempting to change the PH composition of the water we produce. The public was led to believe that there was an attempt to change it into poison. All because one employee noticed something strange going on in the software and reported it....as they were required by law to do.

What transpired after that point was the most unbelievable

episode of false reporting and misinformation I have ever seen in my career, or for that matter, my entire life. It continues to this day, and I promised that someday I would tell the real story of what happened (or didn't), even if it were too late to matter. Here we are.... that day has arrived.

There are still some things I can't say, because our Water Plant is considered critical infrastructure, and providing details about what we run and how we operate it can provide additional ammunition for real cyber criminals to take a shot at us, or as the story was told to the world, take another shot at us (more on that later). It isn't surprising to many that the next BIG cyber-attack would involve the water supply, so while data breaches are damning, an attack that would kill many people is far more terrifying, and more likely to occur soon, or so I thought. As a municipal City Manager, I am responsible for the safety of all our citizens, employees and anyone who consumes any product that we produce. There is no walking away from that, and I have always worried about what would happen if something like I've feared were to occur. When I got the word, I thought my worst nightmare had just come alive.

Because it was Super Bowl weekend, every local, state, and national security agency was in the vicinity, in one form or another. Local Sheriff, FDLE, Homeland Security, Terrorism Task Force, DEP, FBI, you name them. All after the same thing.... catch the bad guy who infiltrated our tiny little utility, and tried, unsuccessfully to change the chemical composition of the water we produce from its normal PH level to that of industrial strength house cleaner. The buzz word used in the Press Conference was LYE, expressed for the visual of what allegedly had happened......ironic, because the story was not true. I don't think we will ever be accused of making it up, and no worries, because once that word was used in the Press Conference, the rest of the worldwide media did it for us (or should I say "to" us).....they made up the remainder of the story, complete with all of the incredibly dangerous things that supposedly happened, or would have happened if our quick thinking employee hadn't prevented

ROLLER COASTERS, REVOLVING DOORS AND REFLUX

the intruder from poisoning the water supply by ultimately stopping the "terrorist" attack. Yes, I said it….and apparently, so did the White House, during a certain period of the aftermath.

Two problems. First, what was reported isn't what happened. Second, what was reported could not have happened.

The effects of the Press Conference would quickly become problematic for me, but more importantly, for my staff. The initial investigation into this "unauthorized intrusion" was done by our Sheriff's department. From what I had been told, they were interviewing all our departmental personnel for over 5 hours, well into the night on Friday, and my staff said that they felt like they were being treated like the perpetrators. To a person, they all felt intimidated by the attitude of the interviewers. Understandable, but not good. If any of us thought that would be all for the weekend attention, we were sadly mistaken. Remember that it was Super Bowl weekend, and the game was close by.

So, for now, let's move on…. over the course of the next week, I spoke to the Sheriff numerous times, since he had been briefed by his investigators on what had allegedly transpired over the weekend, and he was keeping me posted. While we were still trying to understand exactly what occurred (City Administration), the Sheriff told me that he wanted to have a Press Conference on Monday, so that he could get the word out about this "incident," and drive the point home about how this kind of terror is now real, and you all had better re-examine your cyber security protocols, because this could happen to you. A worthy message for certain, so we agreed to participate, and the Mayor and I attended to support the Sheriff and answer any questions. We were totally unprepared for the specifics of what he ended up saying, although I should have been ready, since he did ask me several pointed technical questions throughout the weekend about what some of the reported observations meant. A very reasonable request. Truth be told, at that point in time, I had no reason to believe that what he said during the Press Conference wasn't true. It wasn't until the FBI took over the investigation and concluded that no intrusion occurred that I believe I know what had actually taken place.

We weren't thrilled about telling anyone about the "incident", but we were required by law to report any experience that had the potential to affect any part of our critical infrastructure, and that's exactly what our employees did. So far, the only GOOD news from the reported story was that the "incident" was caught by one of our operators, who instantly took corrective action, rendering the alleged attempt at altering the chemical composition of the water unsuccessful. (This isn't what happened, but the reporting of it saved us from a much larger public debacle, in my opinion). What happened after the Press Conference is what set everything else in motion.

The Sheriff used information provided by his detectives, which was obtained from our Plant personnel, and was not totally accurate, which was our fault. The conclusions drawn about what had happened, along with what it meant, did not come from us. We are responsible for whatever our people told law enforcement, but the conclusions drawn about what really happened, along with what the intended purpose of the incident was not accurately reported by the media. Once again, at that time, we did not know that it wasn't true, we only knew what our Operators saw. The detectives preliminarily decided what they thought it meant.

The Sheriff and I spoke at length about the information shared, after a Conference call with the City Managers and County Administrator, because I thought it was important that he knew that what he had been told was not what occurred, nor could it have been. While he encouraged me to get to the bottom of it, he also stated that he was not going to back off what he said, because the intended message was the same, either way. Public utilities, get your act together, because critical infrastructure terrorism is here, it's real, and here is a live example. Certainly, we had no problem with that message, which has greatly enhanced the resources committed to system security by public and private utilities around the world since February 2021 (including us). You are welcome?

All my employees did was report what they saw, and answer questions posed by Law Enforcement. Unfortunately, the worldwide media reported things that were not true, and drew conclusions about things that did not really occur. I was surprised at hearing some of the specifics mentioned during the Press Conference along with what it meant to the water production process. I had to go back to the Plant and make the Operators show me exactly what they observed, and I did that immediately after the Presser. Up to that point, I had been led to believe (by my own people) that the entire thing was a "non-incident", because the employee reacted so quickly. I should have gathered that information before the Press Conference, but the story, at the time, was that the whole thing turned out to be nothing, so I didn't. In hindsight, another error on my part. Had I visited the Plant before the Press Conference, I might have been able to make sure that the public would know that what was reported could not have occurred. We were not made to look bad in the Press Conference at all (because the "story" was that the "incident" was caught by our employee), but once the worldwide media took it over, we became the press punching bag for municipal utilities across the country, and possibly the world.

Remember... None of this happened. No intrusion. Stay with me, I'm getting to it.

It has been said that we all get our fifteen minutes of fame and boy did I waste mine.... on National TV no less, supporting the Sheriff while he told all who were listening about how an intruder hacked into our Water Plant operating system and attempted to turn the water we produce into a deadly poison, if ingested. If anyone saw the Presser, I think my eyes popped out of my head when I heard the Sheriff go into detail about what had occurred, or at least what he was told had occurred. Not exactly the generic message we thought was going to be shared for the good of the public so that they all review their security protocols. This could happen to any of them, and from what he was told, it has now been attempted.

Next part of the story. While the Global Press is trying to run with this incredible news story and scoop each other, we are being inundated with requests for interviews, from every part of the globe. Fox News, the Wall Street Journal, BBC and a bunch of others that I can't even remember. It was quickly becoming evident that our staff was getting run over with unwanted attention, between the multiple law enforcement and regulatory agencies that all claimed to have jurisdiction over the incident, and the press, who were circulating around the Plant like vultures, waiting for the kill. Pictures (illegal ones), drones, even photos of the wrong Plant were making Local and National News programs. As quickly as I could sense the pressure, my Assistant City Manager and I took control over all inquiries and required that everything go through the City Manager's office, to control the dialogue and take the pressure off the back of the Staff. Through all of this, the Staff operators must continue to function, and produce water. What was worse is that one of our Senior Operators had cancer and had been undergoing treatment for the past two years, occasionally making trips back to his home State to do so. Sadly, shortly after this incident, within about sixty days, he passed away. The hits just kept coming.

Ok, here is the first part of what made this so incredulous. What was described as having happened (the poisoning part) COULD NOT HAVE succeeded. Our system, which was less than ten years old (in the depreciation sense, adolescence), had safety protocols in the water production process, ALL which were working perfectly, and any one of which would have prevented the described disaster from occurring. Let me explain.

First, the observed change in the PH level was really a change in the pump speed that delivers a chemical into the production process. In a normal "batch" of produced water, the amount of this particular chemical would be approximately a "coke can" worth of same, that goes into a test tank that holds 500 gallons of water, before ever getting to the main tank. The alleged intrusion was reported to the public as having altered the dosage of a chemical, specifically into a dangerously high concentration, enough to convert the water's PH into poison. This is where the first mistake was made (although it was based on inaccurate information that our staff provided to the detectives). The alleged access related to the pump speed of how fast the chemical would be injected into the test tank, NOT the actual (dosage) level of the chemical. Upon personally inspecting the reported intrusion, I noted that right underneath the field where this entry was made is a warning sign, in RED letters, that states, "Maximum Pump Speed 200%." This means that regardless of what number was entered into that field, the pump would not exceed 200% of its normal speed, which, by the way, would have injected approximately another coke can's worth of chemical into the (500 gallon) test tank, if it were allowed to occur. Hardly the dosage level reported to have poisoned the good citizens.

Secondly, we remember that the good news here was that our employee noticed the attempt and reversed it before anything changing the dosage level was allowed to occur.... great. In addition to the fact that the employee turned the observed intrusion into a two-minute drill (proving that step #1 in the safety measures worked as it should have), the same employee could have been asleep at the station, and here is what would have happened. ANY entry or system action that alters the PH of the water being produced automatically sets off a series of alarms, to alert the Operator, and the Chief Operator, and the On-call Operator. If NONE of these alarms are answered, the increased chemical level, injected into the test tank, would stop the production of water into the tank. If no one stopped the additional injection of chemical, the Plant would shut down. We have an emergency connection to the County supply, which we can switch over to at any time, with a moment's notice. ALL these safeguards were immediately tested after the incident was reported, and all were in perfect working condition. So, even though what was described is not what happened, the point here is that it couldn't have anyway.

Still asking you to remember.... none of what was reported occurred. Still....

Fast forward to the more current timeframe.... four months later, occasional Press interview requests still occurring, but for the most part, except for letters and articles describing what idiots we are for allowing this to happen, our national exposure calmed down.

We have been somewhat protected from giving out too much information, partially by Florida Statutes, which allows us to exempt information relating to our critical infrastructure from public records, and partially because the "investigation" is still technically open, per the FBI, who took over the investigation.

After a Federal Grand Jury subpoena to the IP vendor, the information was provided to the FBI and the investigation concluded that there was no "intrusion." No evidence that an unauthorized access ever occurred......NONE. Everything that was reported was created by the Press, based on conclusions about what was observed by our employees, and what it would have meant, if it were allowed to occur. The ultimate point here is that it didn't occur....at all.

Back to the origin of the investigation......our employees report what they saw to Law Enforcement, they come out, investigate, draw conclusions about what happened and what it meant (both of which turned out to be inaccurate), and started what seems like a never-ending episode of 60 Minutes.... all for something that didn't even happen.

The FBI will still confirm that there was no intrusion using a third-party program, as the global press had reported, repeatedly. So, what did actually happen? Are we ever going to know?

As I have said before, the intentions of the Sheriff in reporting this to the public is to be applauded. It seems that many utilities around the world all took note, reviewed their protocols and spent tremendous additional amounts on cyber-security as a result. And that is a good thing.

We did too. Not a surprise.

Several legitimate weaknesses in our infrastructure were noted during the investigation and its follow-up, the biggest of which was described as old architecture being used in our network machines. This was true, and although it is simply a limited PC Network, all PCs were still using MS Windows 7 at the time, widely considered outdated and no longer being supported by

ROLLER COASTERS, REVOLVING DOORS AND REFLUX

Microsoft. Our experience had been that Windows 7 worked far better than the subsequent OS efforts (8 and XP, in our opinion, for example), so we were not apologizing for that, we knew that 7 would no longer be supported. Our theory was that we have an IT Staff that can handle anything, and if there was a problem we could not resolve, we would replace the machine and get a new OS at that time.

To summarize, the FBI provided a theory on what they think occurred, and once I knew exactly what had been reported and why, I totally agree with it. One problem, and that is that we will not likely ever be 100% certain, and the FBI will and has documented only that there is "no evidence that a hack or unauthorized access to the City's ROWTP occurred." Because their explanation is just a theory, they cannot document that version of what they think did happen, because it is technically just an opinion. All they can legally conclude is that no hack occurred. I totally accept the fact that the entire incident was my responsibility, and offered to resign several times, even though I had nothing to do with the circumstances that led to the magical Super Bowl weekend and its aftermath (at least the Bucs won). Comes with the territory, and you need to accept that (refer to the section called "If you get run"). Luckily for me, none of the Council members were interested in finding a head to chop off. If they had, that head would have been mine. We have great employees, and they did what they were supposed to do, based on what they observed. What happened for the year after that, will forever be the story of a lifetime, as far as I'm concerned. Hope I get to tell it in greater detail than I've been able to here.

It is worth noting a few things here about leadership in a crisis. I had never experienced a flood of overwhelming press inquiries like this during my career, and it became obvious that it needed to be controlled. As previously mentioned, forcing all press inquiries to come through the City Manager's office turned out to be a wise decision, in retrospect. The employees at the Plant were getting buried with people trying to gain access to anything and everything they could find out about. These people (city employees) can

109

normally go without public contact for a very long time, so it was quickly evident that I needed to do something to take the pressure from them and put it on my office. The incredible skills of my Assistant City Manager, who handled all that subsequent attention with poise and professionalism, significantly reduced the public outcry since then, and continues to even today (she is now the City Manager). From the leadership perspective, taking charge of the situation was required, and once executed, served our organization well.

Another thought about mitigating the damage, which, as I've explained, was not really to the water system, but to our reputation. There was no reason to panic, and over-reacting to the situation was not going to improve it. I had a great number of heartfelt conversations with staff about the alleged incident and found no reason to try and find a scapegoat. The water available to the public was never in danger, our staff did what they were trained to do. While the responsibility for all of it was clearly mine, I don't think it served any purpose in getting excited about it. It sounds cliché to say "Stay cool," but the situation played out in slow motion over the course of the next six months, and we still needed to produce water for our citizens. A plan of attack was required, just as our plan for how to react to the emergency came into play. It wasn't fun, I would be more than happy to admit that, but the dilemma wasn't in figuring out who was responsible from our end. It was how do we manage the public perception of what has been stated about our water system, while still making clean and healthy drinking water for our customers. Add into that equation the pressure on the staff being applied by the media, even for those who worked in other departments. I was keenly aware of what the situation was doing to the mental health of the staff, so I tried to make sure that the Senior managers continued to pay close attention to any employee who might be struggling more so than usual. In order to present to the employees that everything was under control, we had to "Stay Cool." Overall, I think we handled the aftermath well.

I think its appropriate to comment on another aspect of this

ROLLER COASTERS, REVOLVING DOORS AND REFLUX

Reflux contributing "crisis." The incident is an example of something that occurs to Administrators many times and involves things that we have no control over. While you always want to be as aware as you can about things that can and will go wrong, there simply are times where there will be absolutely nothing you can do about it, and that's okay. You always should try to anticipate, but you won't be able to prevent anything and everything from happening. The effort and energy placed into working at understanding those forces, and especially in dealing with the aftermath of whatever does happen, are most important. Because you work in an organization where perception is reality, that may not be enough to protect you from things that could affect your job security, but that fact should not deter you from doing what you can with options available to you at the time a decision is required. That is what makes you a stronger Administrator.

Fast forward to more than a year later, we still get an amazingly high number of international press inquiries, we still answer them the same way, and even though the FBI file is essentially closed on the matter (although not technically closed.... a distinction without a difference?), a lot of good has come out of the experience regarding the financial commitment to cyber-security for critical infrastructure that resulted. I would say that internationally, the Sheriff's intended message was effective. We continue to address our weaknesses, as we have from the outset, although there are not too many overnight fixes. I truly believe that the municipal cyber security world is far better off now than it was on Super Bowl weekend of 2021. Of course, except for the fact that the Bucs didn't repeat as Champs in 2022.

This could easily have been considered in the "Reflections" section but remember this.... the whole incident caused a whole lot of Reflux!!!!

REFLECTIONS

FREE ADVICE FOR PUBLIC ORGANIZATIONS

26

A PAN-WHAT-IC???

No one I've encountered during my career, to this date, can lay claim to having been exposed to a pandemic. From the leadership perspective, this was new territory.... again. Forget about whether someone was trying to poison us through the water supply (or not), this one was far more universal and potentially deadly! Worse yet, no one seems to be able to figure out exactly how you get it! Two years later (and yes, I allegedly just got over it....cost me a cruise) and we still don't know anything about whether masks work, how to get it, what to do when and if you do, how long to stay home and just about everything else. In the leadership context, we learned quite a bit, but maybe not what you might expect. I would have been better off calling this section, "Teaching an old dinosaur new tricks" .... or something like that. Here is what we did learn.

    I didn't miss one day of work, IN THE OFFICE, for the entire time we were in pandemic conditions. My motto was, "I don't lead from the back" .... now, don't get me wrong, I am no hero, but felt strongly that I needed to make sure that everyone knew that the City's leadership was intact and in place, throughout the ordeal. We got through it, or it might be better to say that we are dealing with it still, as best we can, but the things we learned about our staff were quite unexpected. Most importantly, we went through a period where many employees had to go home, and we had to provide them with technology to allow them to function from home. Enter the dinosaur comment…. I had been fighting that battle with certain staff members for at least a year or two prior to the pandemic. Telecommuting was a four-letter word to me, because I always felt that you can't do your job as a public servant if you aren't physically here! I was not a happy camper when telecommuting was thrust upon us. Amazingly, our staff was remarkably resilient and very productive from wherever they were, so shame on me. The dinosaur should have been more open to the thought that this could happen. Stranger still, although maybe only to me, is the fact that most, if not all companies, public and private, allow some version of telecommuting for employees, which has served society very well. Less traffic, better attitudes on the part of employees, among many seeming positives. Silver cloud department, I suppose….no one would wish this pandemic on their worst enemies, but as a result, society has found (by force) a way to allow the work force to function flexibly, and the results have been great. So, what did we learn? Maybe an old dinosaur (me) can learn new tricks.

Leading an organization in this day and age is tough enough, but part of the dance is that you have to be ready for anything, and you can't be too hung up on any one thing. When Covid-19 became common terminology around the world, everything stopped. Then it changed. Now it's different. So has leadership and being a public servant. We still don't exactly know how, because as we emerge from the worst of it, some things are still not the same and others changed, even though we never considered that they would. Some for the better, some not. A new world, for sure. The good news is that you are tougher to judge for whatever you do to display leadership, because no one else has any experience in this regard to draw on. The bad news…. they are going to judge you anyway.

A few other lessons to be learned from the Pandemic experi-

ROLLER COASTERS, REVOLVING DOORS AND REFLUX

ence, as it relates to leadership. The first thing that comes to mind is the importance of being in tune with your personnel's mental health, and that isn't easy. It's always been true, naturally, but nothing like a public health scare that no one has ever faced in their lifetime will bring that point to the forefront more urgently. Especially difficult to lose sight of that need, regardless of circumstances, but more pressing than ever to maintain or develop some kind of consistent way of evaluating how societal things are affecting your personnel. It is one thing to be consistently aware of employee productivity, but it now appears that you will be responsible for understanding the why's of poor performance. There will be a point where you will have to demand accountability, naturally, but the days of simply dismissing poor performers may be gone. Many people think that public organizations were the most lax in this regard anyway, but the recent trend in options for handling poor performance are getting more thorough, and unquestionably more expensive. I think it goes back to part about treating people well in the first place. Keeping morale high keeps turnover low. I've said it before. The pandemic may have taught us that we need to be more creative in understanding how to keep that morale high, and in digging deeper and more thoughtfully into situations where employee productivity is not consistently up to standard. The organization still has all of the same responsibilities to serve the public, but more tools will be needed in the mental health "toolbox", in my opinion.

For young Administrators or those that hope to become one, take a few other things from the lessons we have all learned from the Pandemic. First and foremost, there will be things you have no control over, which we discussed in some detail previously. That is okay. How you handle yourself in those situations is likely to be more important to your success as an Administrator than the percentage of times you successfully avoided crisis.

Secondly, public perception is oftentimes what causes the alleged "crisis." You, as an Administrator, are probably the most knowledgeable about the inner workings for the organization than anyone else, so before you react to the declaration of an emergency by the public, make sure you have all of the important information available to you. I can't tell you how many times the public outcry occurs over something that isn't really a crisis. Point to be made here.... don't over-react, but more importantly, don't react too soon. You may not know exactly what you have on your hands, so don't provide a reaction simply for the sake of being seen as a quick thinker. The pandemic is a great example of a situation where reacting quickly was likely to get you into more trouble than anything, simply because no one really knew how to react at all, not having ever experienced such a thing during our lifetimes. This may have been a situation where my "Herds of Cattle" sub-section (see Roller Coasters) comes in handy, as the Pandemic was the perfect situation to require that you knew what everyone else was doing before deciding what to do in your own organization or community. Tough call to make, but being an effective leader is more important than being the first one to lead, in some situations. I think this was one of them.

While Budgeting for Outcomes seems to be making a comeback, I think this is an excellent spot to discuss Process versus Outcomes. Mechanically, since there are so many situations where you may not control the incident or event, having a consistent approach (or process) to how you will handle the event becomes increasingly important. Please read on...

27

PROCESS VERSUS OUTCOME

As we discussed in an earlier chapter, I steadfastly maintain that you need a process to accomplish about anything these days. One of my best friends in this business said a couple of years ago, "doesn't anyone just wing it anymore?" The answer, without question, is NO. No one does…. these days, you need a plan for about everything.

So, because my plan for this book was to try and help anyone in the "throws" (no idea what that means) of their career, or anyone considering one, I decided to address this concept with the two best personal examples I know of. To have a successful career, it is clearly advantageous to have a plan. Not mandatory, as we know, but certainly likely to increase the odds of success.

For example, go to school, get a degree, discover something you think you'd like to do for a living, and if all of that planning falls into place (the education part), you may have a well-planned career as a result. Of course, we all know that rarely works smoothly, but I wanted to provide an example of how the planning part CAN work in earnest. During my undergraduate studies, we spent an entire month during our senior year in trying to plan and prepare for a career, oftentimes without having a clue about what it might be. That is where the process part comes in.

John Wooden, the "Wizard of Westwood," is the greatest College Basketball Coach of all time. He won 10 NCAA Basketball Championships with the UCLA Bruins, and his philosophy was totally about "process." Jon Cooper, dynamic head coach of the two-time NHL Champion Tampa Bay Lightning, is totally about "process." Their team success has more to do with how they approach the "process" of playing their respective games than it does in focusing on the outcome of any single one of them. It can be very difficult to see how important discipline is in sticking to the process, no matter how the results vary along the way.

Remember the expression, "Success is not a destination, it's a journey." I think that saying is meant to capture the point being made here. To have success, you need to focus on the journey. To quote a personal example, I played College Basketball at a Division II school in Florida (long time ago…there was no 3-point line…okay, stop laughing…. yeah, the shorts were really short, too). Shooting free-throws, thought to be "easy" (after all, they are "free", as in no one is guarding you) is oftentimes very pressure packed, in that they can make the difference in a close game. When you focus on the outcome, that being the desperate need to make them at this crucial point in a game, many players struggle for success. When you focus on the process of good free throw shooting, that being the fundamentals, your ability to concentrate on what represents good form generally increases the likelihood that you will make the shots AND allows you to stop thinking about how important they are, or how you will feel if you miss them. Not overly complicated, but a good example, I think, about how having a process can lead to greater success.

Now, let's talk about Coach Cooper and the Lightning. He has been the coach of the team for the past eight years. Reached a milestone that he didn't want in 2018-19, when the team won the President's Cup for the best record in the regular season (tied for all-time most wins), then proceeded to become the first team in NHL history to win the President's Cup in the regular season,

ROLLER COASTERS, REVOLVING DOORS AND REFLUX

then not win ONE playoff game. Now, you might say what happened to the "process" there? Coach is a "process" kind of guy, and always has been. Interestingly, the skills of his team were challenged by a much more physical bunch of opponents in the playoffs, the officials historically don't call as many penalties in the playoffs as they do in the regular season, they don't play any differently during the playoffs, a few bounces don't go their way, and boom.... they are out of the playoffs after being the favorites going into them. As in life, believe it or not, this isn't a science, but more of an art......and in this case, not only did it not work, but it failed.... miserably! But wait, there is more to the story....

Fast forward to the crazy season that was completed because of the pandemic (let's call it, Bubble Hockey.... enthusiasts will know what that means). For four hundred twenty-two days, Coach Cooper was keeping count of the time needed to show the world that the "process" really does work, after living with the disappointment and introspective shame that goes along with laying such a world renowned "egg" during the previous season. Better still was the fact that his team was playing the same opponent that sent them packing the year before. He believes that when you play the right way (that's the "process"), over the course of time, good things happen to your team, and eventually, those bounces will start to go your way, and no matter what pressure exists, keeping focus on how to play and not the outcome ultimately makes the difference. And this season, boy, did it ever. No matter how many obstacles were presented to the team, Coach's message was the same......stay the course, play the right way, stick to our plan, and the outcome will take care of itself. The boys believed, executed the plan, and now possess the Stanley Cup (twice in a row), which drastically increases each players resume and subsequent value for future career earnings. Not bad.

Back to Coach Wooden for a second. The first book I read about Coach Wooden was a story about how his recruits were amazed when they came to their first practice, and they didn't touch a basketball. Coach Wooden, a master of attention to detail, would spend hours in training his players on how to put on their socks! Crazy, thought NBA Hall of Famer Bill Walton, but genius in that forcing players to pay attention to the "process" of how to play winning basketball started with mastering the art of making sure that you don't get blisters on your feet from wearing your socks incorrectly. It set the tone, limited injuries, and when your best players don't get hurt as often, that usually helps the results. You can imagine what these High School All Americans were thinking at the time, but at the end of the season, when you've just won another National Championship (he won ten), I'm pretty sure that most of the fellas figured out that the socks lesson, was more than just a socks lesson (a metaphor?), and ultimately well worth it. Genius, I'd say......" Process" and detail.

One more example....my best friend and teammate from college is a tremendous Basketball Coach in his own right, but came by it more than honestly, because his dad was one of the all-time greatest College Football coaches ever. He won three National Championships in Division III, and did it without a single scholarship, which makes the achievement incredible on a scale that can't be measured.

In 1990, his Dad's team receives a gift.....a transfer from a Division I school, a real talented Wide Receiver......I had the honor of attending the last National Championship game that the team won, and this kid told a great story at the after party about how he wondered if he had just made a huge mistake coming to this school, because in the first two weeks of practice, they did NOT touch a football once....sound familiar? After winning the Championship, he told the rest of the world that he now understands what that was, and why it works......." process."

Okay, let's bring this to the local government setting. You need rules to live by, which are presented here in another chapter. That is part of the "process" – follow the rules of common sense.

Stick to the "process" .... have one (a plan) .....execute the plan and pay attention to the details. Do so and the results will usually take care of themselves.

28

THE KIDS

My stepdaughter once said to me, "You act conservatively, but you don't think conservatively." I think that was a compliment.

In the professional context, it is obvious, I suppose, that experienced managers must become better and better at dealing with issues associated with leading young people. It seems like a rite of passage that all young people set out to change the world, or at least their little corner of it.

So, how do you lead, knowing that more and more of our workforce is going to be younger than you, and probably disagree with most everything you say or stand for?

Our approach….my "kids" (younger fellow employees) are brilliant. We have been blessed with the smartest bunch of young professionals I've ever been around. I would like to think that isn't by accident.

If I'm trying to explain that using one word, the word would be "smart." We hire smart people. We don't just TRY to hire smart people. We DO it. Smart people can handle many things that get thrown at them, and that is very important today.

To be a little more specific about how, the answer is that we test applicants for most positions. We know that many people have a good line of bull and can wow you in an interview. We are determined to find out how you handle certain situations, whether you are resourceful, easily distracted, and whether you can think under pressure (i.e. - time limits). We don't automatically hire the person who gets the highest grade. We simply use the test as an opportunity to evaluate you further.

If one candidate scores well on the exam, they almost always get the job, especially if the score is far higher than the rest of the applicants. However, if the applicants are all close in score, we may look further into one component of what we need in the position.

By the way, the tests are customized to the requirements of the position. It's another advantage of having smart people. We write our own tests...who better to know what a position will require than the people who have done it, or who will supervise it? They do have general knowledge questions mixed in, but we try to formulate the test as closely to what we are looking for as possible.

This has worked well for us. Very well.

The "Gray area" – It can be difficult to ascertain intellect, or the fit for an applicant to your organization. The best thing you can do is EVERYTHING that is legal to find out what you are getting......Facebook, Linked In, Instagram, Pinterest, Snapchat, call their 3rd grade teacher, whatever......you've heard me say it before, and I'll say it again......the worst thing in organizational effectiveness is TURNOVER (just like in Basketball).....if you hire the wrong person, everything is negatively affected, and it always takes forever to correct the error....heck, sometimes you can't even correct it, which is worse!

The Gray part is that you will NEVER totally know who the right applicant is for the position. You must spend much more effort in trying to figure that out than most companies do.

You CAN'T spend enough time and/or energy in researching what you are going to get in your next hire......it literally can make or break the effectiveness of your department, or worse possibly, the entire organization.

ROLLER COASTERS, REVOLVING DOORS AND REFLUX

Make sure the "kidz" are well-suited to handle what you are going the throw at them, if hired. Energy and resources spent in that pursuit will pay off in the long run.

29

WOMEN ARE MORE EFFECTIVE

Women have no hesitation in making a difficult or unpopular decision, which is the single most important requirement for an effective manager.

Why? Because they don't consider the possibility that whoever is affected by that decision may want to physically hurt them as a response (and they shouldn't).

Men, especially when supervising other men, generally consider the possibility that whoever is affected by a difficult decision, wants to punch them in the face, and may do it. That hesitation can be real and makes men slightly less effective. For some men, it motivates them to make those decisions more directly, because of the feeling of power that comes with that. Ultimately, though, most reasonable men are trying not to be arrogant about using the power.

None of the above speaks to the more current propensity for disgruntled employees to do something far more drastic and dangerous. Another unfortunate sign of the times.

Maybe said another way.... women are more likely to deal with the reality of a situation, even if it will be unpopular? Men tend to want to be liked, and don't want to rock the boat, or get everyone mad at them?

Heck, maybe I'm just speaking for myself......In my organization, 8 of my 10 Department Directors were women.

Whether the real reason is that they are smarter (likely) or just better at it doesn't matter.... what matters is that I am smart enough to know this, and as a result, I relied on a Staff of predominantly women Department Directors.... they never let me down!

30

REALITY IS FOR THE PRIVATE SECTOR

Here is an example of reality, which I've heard really bites (bad reference to a song lyric?).

You work for a company that makes widgets, let's say (channeling my over 30 years of management training.... still have no idea what a "widget" is).

After the most recent monthly close of the books, management determines that they must cut costs to remain competitive in the marketplace, or worse, to remain in business at all.

You are laid off because it was determined that you are not an exceptional "widget" maker. Or worse yet (and more likely), you have the least amount of seniority of anyone in the company.

That is REALITY.

You may be the best widget maker the company has.... doesn't matter. Someone in a decision-making position has concluded that you aren't worth keeping, for whatever reason.

Worst case scenario would likely play out for a company that has shareholders. Every time financial results are required to be reported, adjustments are inevitable, and they CAN affect job security (yours) every single time. Someone must go, because that is the only way that the company can instantly improve the

ROLLER COASTERS, REVOLVING DOORS AND REFLUX

bottom line. Even if the results of that move make everyone else's life more miserable, with more to do to make up for the new vacancy (remember the workload didn't disappear, just the person that was supposed to be doing it), a significant negative affect on productivity will occur. Doesn't matter, someone had to go because the bottom line wasn't good enough.

That is **REALITY**.

Now, here is the Governmental world.

The above example, in theory, does not happen in the Government sector. The Government business model is supposed to be based on how many services the organization can provide for the least amount of taxes. Since there is no Net Income determination required (profit), the reality of people losing their jobs after any accounting period where the entity presents negative financial results are slim, if any.

It's not that government employees can't lose their jobs. I suggest you develop an appreciation for what you have if you choose a government career, because you will have friends and acquaintances in the private sector that are losing their jobs simply because the company didn't make its financial goals for one accounting period. You won't get rich with a career in government, but the aforementioned "reality" won't likely happen to you. I tell my people who have never worked in a government before that they are lucky not to have to work in the "real" world.

REFLECTIONS
FREE ADVICE FOR PUBLIC EMPLOYEES

1 - Go out to lunch…every day you can. No, really, go now. The opportunity to leave your workspace, go outside, anywhere, for thirty minutes, an hour, whatever. It is VITAL to your emotional, physical and psychological well-being. The work is certainly going to be there when you return, but you need to re-charge. Think about something else for a while. Mental health is finally gaining more and more attention, which is a good thing, and long overdue. Since most companies don't give you total discretion on how to approach your workday, here is a simple way to help you cope with whatever the day has brought to your desk. Leave it. For a while, every day if you can.

If you are worried about economics, then bring your lunch each day. Just DON'T eat it at your desk. Go outside, go to the Breakroom, Cafeteria, wherever. Go somewhere else and think, meditate, plan your evening, call your friends, and interrupt their lunchtime! Personally, I have found that going out to lunch was one of the smartest things I've ever done…. mentally. Now, if you have ever seen me, you might be tempted to comment on the sanity of that decision, but that is a different subject. The point here is that the time away, whether it's in a park, a restaurant or even your car, is a positive opportunity to improve (or maintain) your ability to deal with anything that comes your way. A great way to look at them is the way my buddy and I refer to the Back 9 on the golf course, when we play golf. We call them "Half-time Adjustments." Get away, in the middle of your day (or round of golf) and think of how you will approach the second half of it. Think of your lunch break as the opportunity to get away and make "half-time adjustments" to your attitude.... you will come back refreshed, get side issues out of the way, focus, and concentrate on the rest of the day......it works, try it. I'm fat, but my afternoon energy was always good. Okay, get away even if you aren't going to eat.... just go somewhere!

2 – Be friendly, but don't be friends (thanks, Frank). This one is tough, because many of the best people you meet in your life come from interacting with them at work. You will likely spend as much time with them as you do with your own family, which makes it even tougher. The biggest reason this is problematic relates specifically to those becoming or aiming to become managers. If promoted from within, you will go from being one of the gang to being the boss of the gang. Can you handle that? Can they? The desire to improve your situation, which most of us have (we will assume), has you doing everything in your power to get promoted. But have you considered that the toughest part of your new position may be the willingness to lead the employees that used to just be your teammates? The same people you used to complain about the current boss with. See the point? If you know yourself, you may know the answer to this. If you think down deep and are real with yourself, few people will turn down a promotion just because they aren't sure about it. Simply stated, for you and the good of the organization you serve, it's better if you aren't friends with your co-workers. Better for your mental health (if you do get promoted) and better for the organization (decisions made on what's best for the organization versus what's best for your relationships within it). Don't get me wrong, both factors matter, but this isn't a perfect world, very few work situations are, and you are a **PROFESSIONAL** (not enough people take this seriously). You give yourself the best chance of success if you accept this premise as a requirement.

3 - Even though it can be difficult to do, be nicer to your people than you must be. There are certain things that you will have to require as a manager, but I am referring for the most part, to little things. And, of course, some will try to take advantage of your good nature. We consistently point out the need to limit turnover and its negative effect on productivity. Ironically, that discussion has become more important than ever. I believe this is because of the government's reaction to the pandemic. If you are nicer to your people than the rules require (assuming that is possible), you will have more engaged performers working for you, and those people willingly do more than is asked of them. We can all agree to disagree about whether this simply boils down to money (most of the time, I think it does), but there are many things you can do for your staff to let them know you care about them, and sometimes that makes all the difference in the world. Some easy ideas, like Birthday Cards, learning employee family first names, being flexible, allowing leeway on time away from work for medical appointments, refreshment breaks, employee lunches, these are all relatively inexpensive and have been quite effective, in my experience. Anything you can do to let employees know that you care about them usually increases morale and subsequently, performance. Throughout my career, it has consistently amazed me at how much the little things meant to employees. While money is always important, treating employees like they are as valuable as you say they are has a significant effect on their loyalty to you as their manager. Rarely do employees ever complain about the company being nicer than they must be.... try it!

4 – Nicknames are wonderful...everyone should have one. I have been called many things, with most of them being positive, but I am here to suggest that anyone who has given you a nickname is doing you a favor. It means they think you belong! If you can get over the implications of the possible double meanings that can come with it. It's the simplest tangible evidence that you are part of the gang, the team, the fellas, the women, the group that gets things done!

I encourage you to embrace giving nicknames and be thankful for those you may receive....it means you belong and that should be a wonderful boost to your wellbeing.... if taken in the proper context. I realize that nicknames can be hurtful, but if you perceive them as positive in those you receive, and are kind in those you give to others, it's all good. You are making the world a better place. In the world we are now living in, there is danger in suggesting nicknames for others in the workplace, and I guess I must acknowledge this. The point is simply not to take yourself so seriously that others consider you to be aloof. Enjoy the attention! From my experience, I usually use last names (old childhood memory from how many Little League coaches butchered the pronunciation of my last name), ask their permission (very few people have a problem with it), or in cases, we use their email names, which make for entertaining nicknames when put together phonetically.

It had been said that in my twenty-eight years of basketball coaching, my skill in giving nicknames far outweighed my ability to coach. I hope that wasn't true, but I loved the suggestion that nicknames I provided to the kids I've coached over the years have largely stuck with them.

As you know, I had a nickname that stuck with me from High School, throughout my life.... there will be a quiz at the end of this book, to see if you read it thoroughly. My nickname is in there somewhere! Maybe even more than once!

5 – Don't forget where you came from – It's an old saying, yet an important one....I would go so far as to say that I think you should keep a list. And use it. Not only is it a nice thing to occasionally reach out and acknowledge someone who has helped you along the way, but it vastly improves every life that is included in the "process." The recipient of the communication feels better about themselves, and probably feels empowered by having been recognized. Even just a phone call on occasion does wonders. The 'fabric of civilized society'.... we all need people, more so than ever!

Always wanted to be a rock star and have someone ask me who my "influences" were.... well, no rock stardom, and you didn't ask to see it, but I do have a list. The people that influenced me along the way, turned me into whatever I am, for better or worse. I've got to tell you that I loved doing it. A way to thank anyone and everyone that influenced my life, in some little way.

Saying 'Thank you' – by no means complete, but I try to evaluate my journey as often as possible, and it is impossible to do so without realizing how many people helped me along the way. I want people to know how much they meant to me...not in writing this book necessarily, but during my journey. I may be a blankety blank (enter your own choice of adjective here) to many, but the point is that whatever I am, I understand and appreciate how important it is to learn from people encountered along the way.

6 – Be a Teacher/Coach/Mentor – for much of the same rationale I just mentioned, it's important for you to help others develop their skills, no matter what the subject. I can personally attest that there is NO more rewarding feeling than what you get when you help someone else get better at something. I never won a State Championship in my twenty-eight years of coaching high school basketball, but the rush you get when you see someone succeed or improve based on input and/or experience you've provided is unbeatable.... try it, you'll like it (Hey, Mikey!!!....he likes it!!! Old Cereal commercial reference).

7 – Educate Public Officials (Civics 191) – you may never get the chance to do this, but be cautioned that if you ever do, you MUST take advantage of it! As previously discussed, part of what is RIGHT about Public Service is the altruistic part.... helping other people, helping build communities, and helping people to realize how much they are a part of all the wonderful things. Just like in team sports, when they are all working in tandem, it is a beautiful thing to behold.

Unfortunately, many Public Officials have a badly distorted view of what their roles are, and that is why you must try to get newly elected officials to realize that their role is strictly limited to policy, not operations. Naturally, like everything else in government, the distinction between the two is…. you guessed it…. NOT black and white…..it's gray, like everything else.

8 - Create policies that make actual sense – if you ever become a manager, you will have a bigger role in this than you will in most other roles you may get to play. As I've tried to explain previously, many policies in every level of government do not make any sense, either practically or economically. The worst part of politics is that any time this occurs, elected officials look to add layers of fix to the problem, which almost invariably makes the problem more convoluted and ultimately worse. Policies do not need to be ultra-complex; they just need to be easy to interpret and follow. If we'd stay in our lanes and stick to the basics, I think the effectiveness of government could be drastically better than it is, for the most part. Don't forget to look for the examples, however, of where it continues to be done the way it should…. they do exist and you can find them!

9 – Term limits – There certainly are variants of this that can work, but I think it's fair to say that any elected official that makes a decision based on the hope that its popularity will get he/she re-elected is already violating the intent of what Public Service should mean to them. If we have term limits, that can be limited. Period.

THE FINISH LINE

31

IT'S OVER

Wow, it's really over.... the book.... okay, my career, too.... hopefully those are the only two things on the list, for now.

I know that these are underwhelming, in that they are not earth shaking, paradigm changing suggestions that need to be part of how we can make organizations better, ourselves more successful (and possibly marketable). Hope you aren't too disappointed to find out that wasn't really the reason I wrote the book. I've always enjoyed the aspect of teaching and coaching as it relates to relevance, but also thoroughly enjoyed being in front of those who thought I had something to say. As my career grew, through many bosses, mentors, and people that influenced my development, I began to think I could write....and, to a degree, entertain in the "process." Obviously, the reader will decide if any of that is true. If you've made it this far in the book and haven't thrown it out yet, then I will consider that a good sign. I hope that this was a good read, and never lost too much track of the intended overarching themes, meaning the need to excel at whatever you attempt, without beating yourself up too much along the way, and having some fun. Remember that this project was the result of a promise I made to my mom, as much as anything. I hope that I've contributed something you can use, so that you think this was worth your time in reading. Trust me, even from above, my mom is critiquing it all the way through, in every category!!!!!

32

EMBRACING IRRELEVANCE

Now that it's over, I must deal with the sensitive (for me) subject of relevance.

Relevance has always been an important part of my life. I suspect that to be true for many others but can't speak for anyone else. One of the greatest joys of being a parent is related to the fact that you are relevant to those you have created, although I'm sure it doesn't feel like that all the time. For as long as you live. I know, double-edged sword.

While I have an incredible Stepdaughter, having no natural children of my own may be why I feel that relevance is so important. To have a fulfilling life, you need to be vital to someone or something. It can be as simple as an animal, who lives and dies for your happiness (humans would be wise to take that lesson). In the context I am referring to here, it has always been important to me, to be important to others. One of the best experiences of my life was coaching HS Basketball, which I did as a labor of love for twenty-eight years. Talk about relevance. For all that time, a group of high school kids depended on me for basketball, but also for life lessons. My coaching record may not be anything to write home about, but the rewards that I received for being in that position were life-sustaining, motivating and wonderfully positive.... for me. Naturally, I hope they were for those who played for me, as well.

As I head into the sunset professionally, it occurs to me that my position as a City Manager carried with it a certain relevance factor, that will now be disappearing. What am I going to do about that? I'm very excited about the prospect of not having any more "school nights" but doing some soul searching about how to handle the change. Irrelevance looms large, I'm afraid.... I'm hoping to come up with ways to stay busy, so that I either remain relevant somehow, or stay so busy that I don't think about it! Stay tuned! I'll let you know how it goes.

I am leaving this profession at the best time possible; it would seem. From my lens, I was finally on a team (and blessed to have been able to lead it) that has great experience, mad skills, and most importantly, doesn't work in silos (see Reflux section). The willingness to collaborate and help your teammates is the most important thing you can have in a high-performing organization. The one I am leaving has it....in abundance! It is such a great feeling to have worked alongside so many talented and caring professionals. If there was a Public Service "Woodrow Wilson Cup", for example (the King of Public Administration?), I'd bet my lunch money that the organization I am leaving would be strong contenders for it (and we have established how much I really like lunch)!

CLOSING

If I were to summarize the basics of what I hope you take from this book personally, I would say:

Be yourself.

Don't beat yourself up.

Don't lie to yourself.

Try to be true to what you know about yourself when picking a career path or move.... the money won't mean as much as you think it will.... you make do with what you have, you always do and always will.

Be great with people.... whatever that means to you is all that matters.... if you are, other people will know it, and they are the ones that will judge.

Your attitude will mean more than anything else you do throughout your career....be grateful for having a career, those are the people that have the most successful ones.

If you read this book, and I can help you in any way, please call on me. Heck, even if you didn't read this book, if I can help you in any way, call on me. I've been called fat, out of shape, dumb, incompetent, the best coach on the planet, and a bunch of other things in my life.... most of which are true (you decide). The one thing NO ONE has ever called me is dishonest….and I am most proud of that. In this day and age, you can rely on fewer and fewer people who willingly deliver that honesty. You may not want to hear any and everything I've got to say, but I can promise you complete honesty in whatever I do say…. there will never be any sugar coating it…. you deserve better than that. The truth is becoming a lost art, in every walk of life…. there is that "gray" crap again.

Best to all of you…. I'll be around, trying to be relevant somehow…

NOTES

The Allure of Public Service

1. *"Who Moved My Cheese?"*, Spencer Johnson, M.D., published in 1998, 2002, G.P. Putnam's Sons.
2. *"What Color Is Your Parachute?"* Richard N. Bolles with Katharine Brooks, published multiple times, most recently in 2022, Ten Speed Press.
3. *"Confessions of a Basketball Junkie."* Dirk Dunbar, published in 2015, Outskirts Press, Inc.

ABOUT THE AUTHOR

Al Braithwaite, 65, has lived in Pinellas County for 45 years, after growing up in Commack, New York, a suburb of the Big Apple, half-way out on Long Island. In fact, dead middle of Long Island, if you look at a map, half-way between the Long Island Sound and Fire Island. Great place to grow up.

After two years of northern weather while in college, he decided to come to St. Petersburg and attend Eckerd College. After receiving a bachelor's degree in '79, he only knew that he wanted to stay in the area and turned down several management opportunities elsewhere to do so. The attraction of living near Pass-a-Grille Beach was too much to resist.

Career-wise, he started out teaching HS Algebra in a small private school owned and operated by Dr. Thomas V. Howard, Jr., a well-known educator in the St. Petersburg area. After six years of trying to inspire kids to love math, he took a summer job with the City of Madeira Beach, and, as they say, the rest is history. This book is meant to summarize that history.

Al is married to his wife and best friend, Carlajean, whom he met during his tenure in Madeira Beach in 1987. Carla is the backbone of all things that get done in the Braithwaite household. For these 37 years of government service, 28 of which were simultaneously shared as a high school basketball coach, she has been everything from a coach's wife (some suggest widow) to the Administrative first lady of the City Manager's office.

Al's family includes one daughter, Stacey, who is married to

Matt and has three wonderful children, Finley, Nick and Sonny. His passions are grandchildren, all things hockey and the Tampa Bay Lightning. He lives in Oldsmar, Florida and occasionally in Cleveland, Tennessee.

www.ingramcontent.com/pod-product-compliance
Lightning Source LLC
Chambersburg PA
CBHW072018110526
44592CB00012B/1353